Better Homes and Gardens®
STEP-BY-STEP

Wiring

Better Homes and Gardens® Books
Des Moines, Iowa

Better Homes and Gardens® Books
An imprint of Meredith® Books

Step-by-Step **Wiring**
Editor: Benjamin W. Allen
Associate Art Director: Tom Wegner
Copy Chief: Angela K. Renkoski
Electronic Production Coordinator: Paula Forest
Editorial Assistant: Susan McBroom
Design Assistant: Jennifer Norris
Production Manager: Douglas Johnston
Prepress Coordinator: Marjorie J. Schenkelberg

Meredith® Books
Editor in Chief: James D. Blume
Managing Editor: Christopher Cavanaugh
Editor, Shelter Books: Denise L. Caringer
Director, New Product Development: Ray Wolf
Vice President, General Manager: Jamie L. Martin

Better Homes and Gardens® **Magazine**
Editor in Chief: Jean LemMon
Executive Building Editor: Joan McCloskey

Meredith Publishing Group
President, Publishing Group: Christopher Little
Vice President and Publishing Director: John P. Loughlin

Meredith Corporation
Chairman of the Board and Chief Executive Officer: Jack D. Rehm
President and Chief Operating Officer: William T. Kerr
Chairman of the Executive Committee: E. T. Meredith III

Produced by Greenleaf Publishing, Inc.
Publishing Director: Dave Toht
Associate Editor: Steve Cory
Assistant Editor: Rebecca JonMichaels
Design: Melanie Lawson Design
Illustrations: Bob Stocki, Art Factory
Technical Consultants: Gordon Ehorn; Unity Electric, Inc., St. Charles, Illinois; Joe Hansa

Cover Photograph: Tony Kubat Photography

All of us at Better Homes and Gardens® Books are dedicated to providing you with information and ideas you need to enhance your home. We welcome your comments and suggestions about this book on wiring. Write to us at: Better Homes and Gardens® Books, Do-It-Yourself Editorial Department, LN-112, 1716 Locust St., Des Moines, IA 50309–3023.

Note to the Reader: Due to differing conditions, tools, and individual skills, Meredith Corporation assumes no responsibility for any damages, injuries suffered, or losses incurred as a result of following the information published in this book. Before beginning any project, review the instructions carefully, and if any doubts or questions remain, consult local experts or authorities. Because local codes and regulations vary greatly, you always should check with local authorities to ensure that your project complies with all applicable local codes and regulations. Always read and observe all of the safety precautions provided by any tool or equipment manufacturer, and follow all accepted safety procedures.

TABLE OF CONTENTS

INTRODUCTION

Many do-it-yourselfers who wouldn't think twice about building a bunk bed or framing a wall will shrink at the prospect of electrical work. Frantic questions spring to mind: "How do I know the power is really off when I'm working on it?" "If I make a mistake, will I burn the house down or injure someone?" So they call in a professional electrician for even the simplest repairs and pay top dollar for work they could have done themselves.

Make no mistake: Electricity deserves respect. But if you are equipped with a basic understanding of how electricity works, and if you follow instructions that emphasize safety, you can successfully complete most home electrical projects.

Safety is indeed the most important consideration when approaching a wiring job. In most cases, a flip of a circuit breaker and a quick test of the wires for power—10 minutes of work at most—will ensure that you can't receive an electrical shock as you work.

The fact is, electricians spend most of their workday performing tasks that a competent homeowner could do just as well, although probably not as quickly. In fact, for many remodeling installations, the majority of the work lies in opening and covering up walls before and after the actual electrical work—which is more plastering and redecorating than wiring.

Step-by-Step Wiring explains how your electrical system works and what it takes to tackle most household repairs and improvements. It shows you, in step-by-step fashion, how to fix minor and major problems and how to install new electrical circuits and devices in a professional manner.

Perhaps best of all, *Step-by-Step Wiring* will help you evaluate what you can take on yourself. You'll find that many electrical repairs and improvements are things you can do. If you choose to call in the pros, you'll be equipped to manage the job wisely.

Working to Code

Even though you are a do-it-yourselfer working on your own house, you have the same responsibilities as a licensed electrician. You must install electrical systems that will remain safe for many decades. That means using only those techniques and materials that are acceptable to the building codes of your area.

Local codes vary from place to place, but are based on the National Electrical Code (NEC), published by the National Fire Protection Association, a nonprofit agency. The NEC covers just about every conceivable electrical situation. The procedures in this book represent the editors' understanding of the NEC.

Always check with your local building department if you are considering adding or changing your wiring in any substantial way, or if your existing electrical service looks like it may be substandard. Electrical codes may seem bothersome at times, but they are designed to protect homeowners and keep a home's electrical system running smoothly.

Working with Your Local Building Department

If you're planning to extend an existing circuit or add a new one, you may need to apply to your building department for a permit and arrange to have the work inspected. Local officials can tell you about this and explain what jobs require the involvement of a licensed electrician.

If you will be adding new service—not just replacing one fixture with another one—check with your building department before proceeding. Neglecting to do so could cause you the expense and trouble of tearing out and redoing your work.

There's no telling what kind of inspector you will get: He or she could be helpful, friendly, and flexible, or a real stickler. But no matter what sort of personality you'll be dealing with, your work will go better if you follow these guidelines:

■ This book is a good place to start, but learn as much as you can about each project before you talk with an inspector from your local building department. That way, you'll be able to avoid miscommunication and get your permits more quickly. Your building department may have literature concerning your type of installation. If not, consult the NEC.

■ Go to your inspector with a plan to be approved or amended; don't expect the building department to plan the job for you.

■ Present your plan with neatly drawn diagrams and a complete list of the materials you will be using.

■ Be sure you clearly understand when you need to have inspections. Do not cover up any work that needs to be inspected.

■ Be as courteous as possible. Inspectors are often wary of homeowners. Show the inspector you are serious about doing things the right way, and comply with the requirements without arguing.

How to Use This Book

*B*egin by reading the first section, "Getting to Know Your System." This will give you a firm base of general knowledge that will help you understand specific parts of your electrical system. If you plan to do some electrical work yourself, read the pages of the next section, "Tools and Materials," that apply to your project. Next read those pages in the "Skills" section that apply to the job you have in mind. For instance, if you are replacing a light fixture, you'll want to read "Stripping Wire" and "Connecting Wires," but you can ignore other skills until you take on another project.

Consult "Troubleshooting and Repairs" to see how to rewire lamps and plugs, repair light fixtures, test and replace switches, and fix almost anything else that can go wrong with your wiring and fixtures. If you want to install new electrical fixtures and service—anything from a new ceiling light to a completely rewired room—you'll find instructions in this book. In "Improvements" you'll learn how to install a variety of lights and switches, run telephone and cable line, and improve your home's safety with GFCI receptacles and breakers.

Don't be afraid to think big. If you have the time and energy, there is virtually no electrical installation you cannot make. This book presents step-by-step instructions that ensure your success for the most complicated projects—wiring three-way switches, installing switched receptacles and outdoor service, and even planning and adding whole new circuits.

Feature Boxes

*I*n addition to basic instructions, you'll find plenty of tips throughout the book. For every project, a You'll Need box tells you how long the project will take, what skills are necessary, and what tools you must have. The other tip boxes shown on this page provide practical help to ensure that the electrical work you do will be as pleasurable as possible, and that it will result in safe and long-lasting improvements to your home.

MEASUREMENTS

Keep an eye out for this box when standard measurements or special measuring techniques are called for.

Money $ Saver

Throwing money at a job does not necessarily make it a better one. Money Saver offers smart ways to accurately estimate your material needs and make wise purchases.

EXPERTS' INSIGHT

Tricks of the trade can make all the difference in helping you do a job quickly and well. Experts' Insight gives insiders' tips on how to make the job easier.

CAUTION!

When a how-to step requires special care, Caution! warns you what to watch out for. It will help keep you from doing damage to yourself or the job at hand.

TOOLS TO USE

If you'll need special tools not commonly found in a home-owner's toolbox, we'll tell you about them in Tools to Use.

HOW CIRCUITS WORK

*E*lectricity is the flow of electrons through a conductor. In home electrical systems, wires, consisting of highly conductive copper wrapped in insulation for safety, are the conductors—the assigned pathway through which the electricity travels. A host of other items—a fork, a screwdriver, yourself—also can serve as conductors, sometimes with disastrous results. It's the goal of a safe electrical system to prevent this from happening.

Electricity always flows in a loop, known as a circuit. When a circuit is interrupted at any point, the electricity shuts off. As soon as the circuit is reconnected, the flow begins again.

Electricity is generated by your local electric company. Overhead and underground wires bring power from the utility company lines to a home's service head, also called a weatherhead because it can withstand wind, heat, and ice. Although the utility company sends high-voltage electricity along some of its power lines, by the time it reaches your house, it is 120 volts per wire.

The electricity passes through an electric meter, which measures how much enters the house. It proceeds to a service panel (also called the breaker box or fuse box), which distributes electricity throughout the house along individual circuits. Each circuit flows out of the service panel, through a number of fixtures and receptacles, and back to the service panel. (For more on service panels, see pages 8–9.)

To make a circuit, electricity is carried out of the service panel on "hot" wires that usually have black insulation, although they sometimes may be red, and is returned to the panel on neutral wires that have white insulation.

The service panel contains

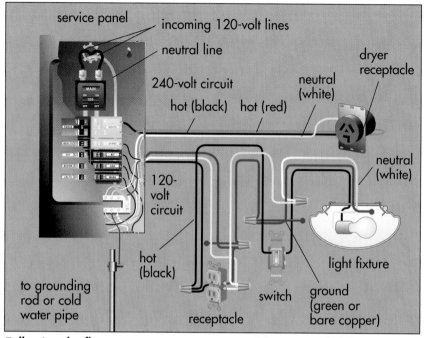

Following the flow

The flow of electricity in typical household circuits starts with the two 120-volt lines and single neutral line that enter the top of the service panel. Both 120-volt lines are used to make the 240-volt circuit, though only one

circuit breakers or fuses—both are safety devices that shut off the power in case of a short circuit or other fault in the circuit (see pages 8–9, 61–62).

Each circuit has a number of outlets that lead to smaller circuits through which the electricity flows. These outlets might include receptacles, fixtures, and switches. For example, a wall switch interrupts (off) or completes (on) the circuit to one or more light fixtures. Some heavy-use appliances—such as a dishwasher, disposal, or microwave oven—may need a circuit to themselves.

Most circuits carry current of 120 volts, which, while it will give you quite a jolt, will not seriously harm most people if they should accidentally come into contact

neutral line is needed for the electricity to complete its loop. The 120-volt circuit has one hot wire (black) and one neutral wire (white), plus a copper ground wire (green). In case of a short, the ground wire carries the current safely into the ground.

with it. Most homes also have one or two 240-volt lines, which use two hot wires and one neutral wire to double the power. Because of the higher power, take special care when dealing with these.

Every electrical system must be grounded for safety. Usually this is done by connecting a wire to a cold water pipe, to a grounding rod sunk deep into the ground, or sometimes to both. Grounding allows excess current to travel harmlessly into the earth in case of overload or a short circuit.

Circuits in your home may be grounded with a grounding wire that is bare copper or green, or they may be grounded by means of the metal receptacle boxes and the metal sheathing that contains the wires (see page 10).

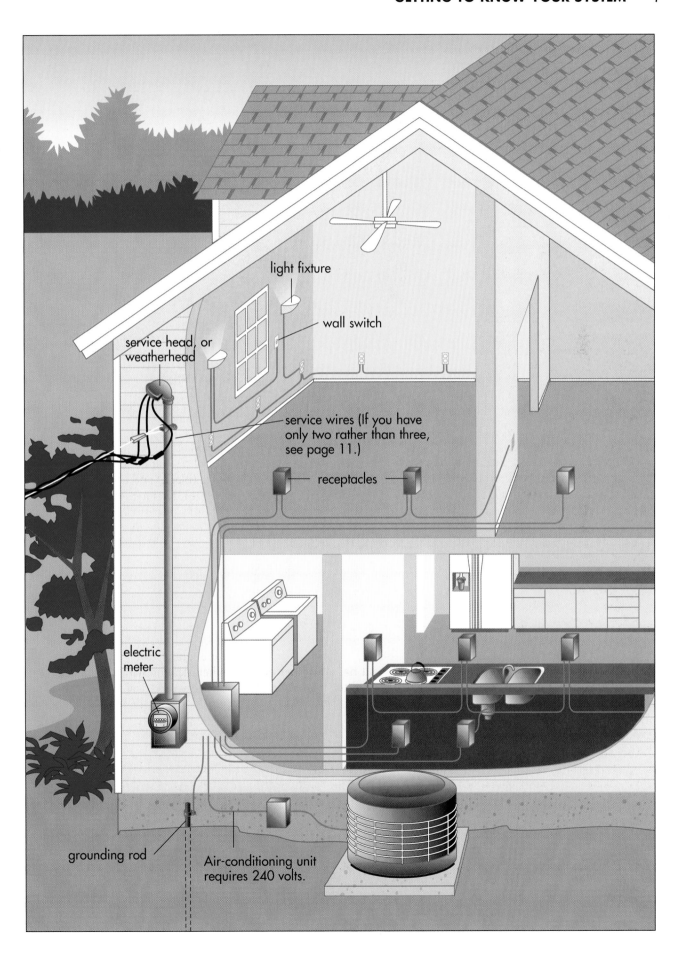

light fixture

wall switch

service head, or
weatherhead

service wires (If you have
only two rather than three,
see page 11.)

receptacles

electric
meter

grounding rod

Air-conditioning unit
requires 240 volts.

SERVICE PANELS

Electrical projects always begin at the service panel, which is either a breaker box or a fuse box. When a short or an overload shuts down power to a circuit, this is where you go to restore the flow. It's also where you cut off power to a circuit before starting a project.

Power arrives from the meter through two main power wires, each of which carry 120 volts of electricity into the house. Usually, these are black and/or red. In addition, there is a white main neutral wire, which carries electricity back to the utility. The main hot wires are connected to a main power shutoff. When you turn this off, you don't de-energize the hot wires, but you cut power to everything else in the box.

Breaker boxes

Emerging from a breaker box's main shutoff are two hot bus bars. The 120-volt breakers are each attached to one of these bars. (This means that if one of the main hot wires gets damaged outside your house, you will lose power to about half of the circuits in your house.) Each 240-volt breaker is attached to both bus bars, giving them twice the power. When a circuit is overloaded or a short occurs, the breaker trips and shuts off power before the wires heat up and become a danger.

The main neutral wire is connected to the neutral bus bar. This bar is connected to a system ground wire, which leads to a grounding rod. White wires for every circuit, and possibly bare or green ground wires, also connect to the neutral bus bar. As a result, each 120-volt circuit has a black or colored wire leading from a circuit breaker, a white wire leading to the neutral bus bar, and possibly a bare copper or green-covered ground wire also connected to the neutral bar. Each 240-volt circuit has two wires leading to a circuit breaker. In addition, the 240-volt circuit has a neutral and, possibly, a ground wire, connected to the neutral bus bar. Systems with conduit or armored cable do not need separate ground wires—the conduit or metal sheathing act as ground conductors.

For how to troubleshoot the several types of circuit breakers and how to check for the cause of shorts, see page 61.

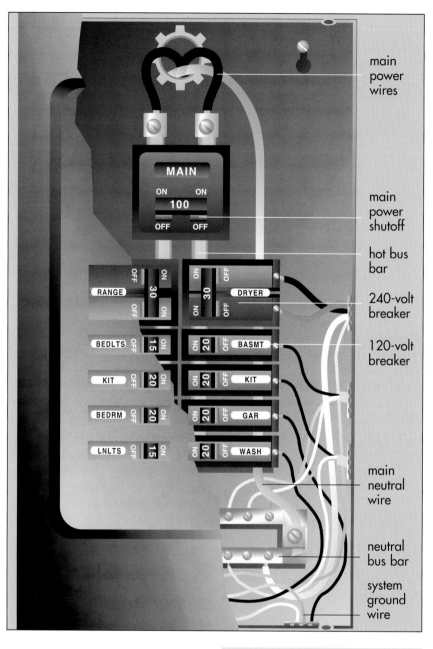

main power wires

main power shutoff

hot bus bar

240-volt breaker

120-volt breaker

main neutral wire

neutral bus bar

system ground wire

CAUTION!
LEAVE INCOMING WIRES FOR THE UTILITY COMPANY
If you suspect that the wires entering your house may be damaged in any way, do not attempt to work on them yourself. Have the utility company inspect them. Usually they will inspect and repair them for free.

Fuse boxes

If you have an older home that has not been rewired in the last 25 or 30 years, chances are that its electrical heart is a fuse box rather than a breaker box.

Fuse boxes are wired and work the same way as breaker boxes (see page 8), but instead of tripping as a breaker does, a fuse "blows" when there's too much current in its circuit. When this happens, you must eliminate the short or the overload, remove the blown fuse, and screw in or plug in a new one.

As with a breaker box, power comes in through two main power wires. (In a house with no 240-volt equipment, there may be only one of these.) Current flows through a main disconnect, in this case, a pullout block that holds a pair of cartridge fuses.

Next in line are a series of plug fuses that protect the black hot wires of the individual circuits, often called branch circuits. Unscrewing a fuse disconnects its circuit. A neutral bus bar receives the main neutral wire as well as all the neutral wires for the branch circuits. A system ground wire leads from the neutral bus bar to a grounding rod outside the house.

For tips on troubleshooting a fuse box, see page 62.

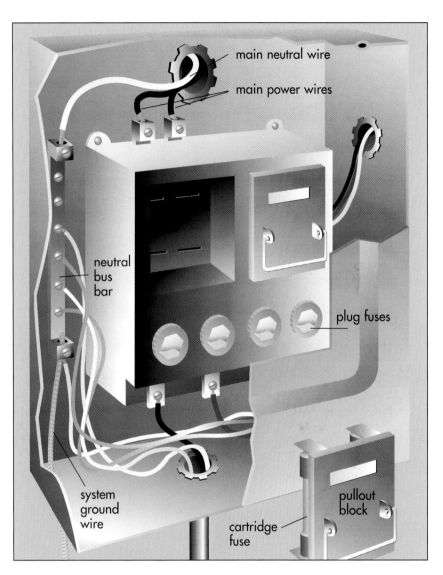

main neutral wire

main power wires

neutral bus bar

plug fuses

system ground wire

cartridge fuse

pullout block

> **CAUTION!**
> NEVER "UPGRADE" A FUSE
> If you have a chronically overloaded circuit, you might be tempted to install a bigger fuse—replace a 15-amp fuse with a 20-amp fuse, for example. Don't do it. Wiring that gets more current than it was designed to handle heats up and can catch fire. Always replace a blown fuse with one of the same amperage rating.

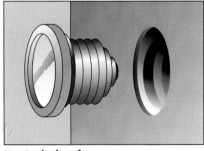

Typical plug fuse
A plug fuse is threaded and screws into the fuse box. Handle only the rim. Do not touch the threads while removing or replacing the fuse. For information on identifying and replacing a blown fuse, see page 62.

Handling pullout blocks
Larger 240-volt circuits, as well as main shutoff fuses, often are protected by pullout blocks that contain cartridge fuses. If you need to pull out a cartridge fuse that is not in a pullout block, do not use your fingers. Get a fuse puller (see pages 15 and 62).

GROUNDING AND POLARIZATION

Older homes often have receptacles and fixtures that are ungrounded, and many local codes do not require that they be rewired so they're grounded. Still, grounding is worth adding to your system because it adds protection against electrical shock. Grounding provides a third path for electricity to travel along, so if there is a leak of any sort, it will flow into the earth rather than into the body of a person who touches a defective fixture, appliance, or tool.

An electrical system is grounded with a grounding rod driven at least 8 feet into the ground outside the house or connected to a cold water pipe. Each individual branch circuit must be grounded as well, either with a separate wire that leads to the neutral bar of the service panel or with metal sheathing that runs without a break from each outlet to the panel. (In theory, electrical outlets can be grounded individually, but this is impractical.)

In some locations of your house—especially where the outlet and/or appliances may become wet—ground-fault circuit-interrupter (GFCI) receptacles are required (see pages 76–77). Older, ungrounded circuits usually are protected by polarization, which is less effective than grounding but better than nothing. Grounded and polarized receptacles work only if they are wired correctly. See pages 58–59 to test for this.

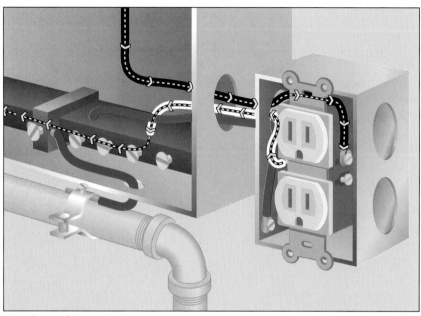

A polarized receptacle
A polarized outlet has one slot that is longer than the other. This is to ensure that the plug is inserted so that hot current flows through black or red wires, and neutral current flows through white wires. Although not as safe as a grounded system, polarization is the next best thing.

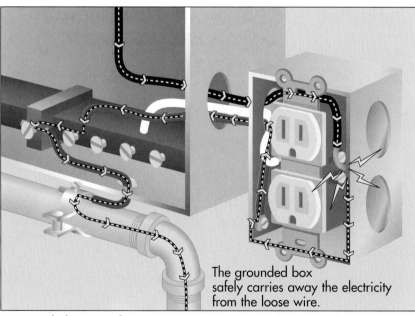

The grounded box safely carries away the electricity from the loose wire.

A grounded receptacle
The grounding circuit must follow an unbroken path to the earth. A third, rounded prong on modern plugs fits into the round slot in the receptacle. This slot connects to a wire—or to metal conduit or sheathing—that leads without interruption to the neutral bus bar of the breaker box. The system ground wire then leads from the bus bar to the earth. Often a cold water pipe is used for grounding instead of a grounding rod, because it is connected to water supply pipes that go deep under the ground.

CAUTION!
DON'T ALTER PRONGS ON PLUGS
Never clip or file down the prongs on a grounded or polarized plug. Go to the heart of the problem: Test and upgrade your circuit and receptacle.

LIMITATIONS OF OLDER SYSTEMS

An older home may have electrical service that is inadequate or even unsafe. It can be confusing as well. If you are unsure about your home's wiring, have a professional check it out.

Some older systems have only two wires—a hot and a neutral—entering the house, rather than three. This means that you will not be able to have any 240-volt circuits for large appliances.

Modern electrical service provides at least 100 amps of power, which is enough to power a medium-size house with an average number of appliances. A house built in the 1950s or before may only have 30-amp service (the circuit box will have only two fuses) or 60-amp service (four fuses). With so few circuits, the number of fixtures and appliances you can run will be limited.

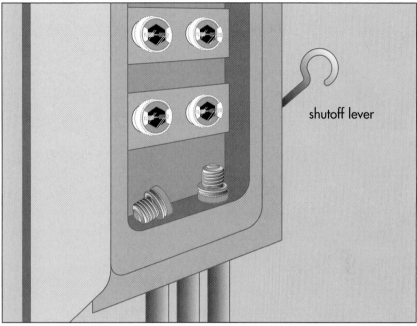

Limited service
This 60-amp service panel contains four 15-amp fuses and a switch lever for shutting off power.

If you have this or a 30-amp (two-fuse) box, it's a good idea to have a professional upgrade you to a 100-amp service panel with breakers.

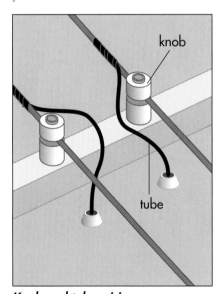

Knob-and-tube wiring
This type of wiring was common in houses built before World War II. The individual wires are wrapped in a rubberized cloth and have no additional protection. There is no ground wire. These wires should be replaced with modern cable, particularly in areas where they are exposed, such as attics and basements.

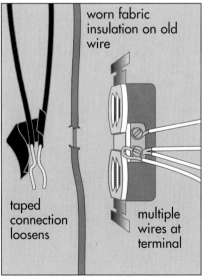

Sources of shorts and faults
Loose taped wires, old wire damaged because it's exposed, and multiple wires slipping off a single terminal screw may seem minor, but can have drastic consequences. The consequences, such as fire and electrocution, are the reasons codes are strict about good wiring practices. See pages 29–31 for the correct way to connect wires.

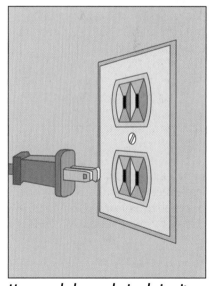

Ungrounded, unpolarized circuits
If your outlets have two slots that are the same size, then they are neither polarized nor grounded (see page 10). This leaves you with no protection against shocks from defective fixtures or appliances using that outlet. At the very least, you need to install polarized outlets (see pages 58–59).

HOUSEHOLD CIRCUITS

*T*he electrical service in your house is divided into branch circuits, each of which supplies power to a defined area of your home. It is important to make sure that no branch circuit is carrying too great a load, or you will be constantly resetting breakers or replacing fuses. Some appliances need to have a circuit for themselves. An electric stove or dryer will have its own 240-volt circuit; other heavy-use appliances may require their own 120-volt circuits. More often, a circuit supplies a number of outlets, using a range of power.

To find out if a circuit is overloaded, add up the total power drawn by the circuit as outlined below. Check the breaker or fuse to see how many amps the circuit can deliver. If your total use exceeds the amperage the circuit can supply, change your usage. The solution may be as simple as plugging an appliance into a different receptacle—or you may have to add another circuit to your electrical system.

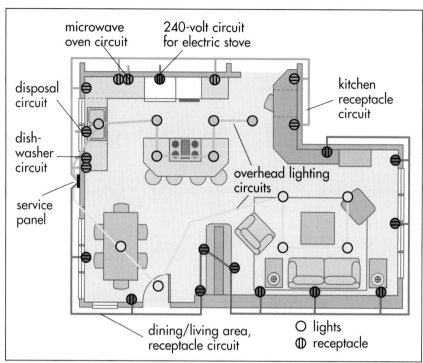

Typical circuit plan
A well-planned electrical system will have branch circuits that serve easily defined areas or purposes. Unfortunately, many homes—especially if they have been remodeled by do-it-yourselfers—have circuits that roam all over the house. Note that some appliances, such as the microwave oven, dishwasher, and disposal, have their own circuits. The electric stove has its own 240-volt circuit. Otherwise, circuits are roughly organized by the rooms they serve and their anticipated demand.

MEASUREMENTS

To figure your circuit loads, total the watts being used. Check the specification label on each appliance. Also note the wattage of the lightbulbs in fixtures on the circuit. Divide the total by 120 (the number of volts). The resulting number will tell you how many amperes ("amps") the circuit draws when all appliances and lights are on—and whether or not you are placing too great a demand on it. Here are some typical watt and amperage figures for common household appliances.

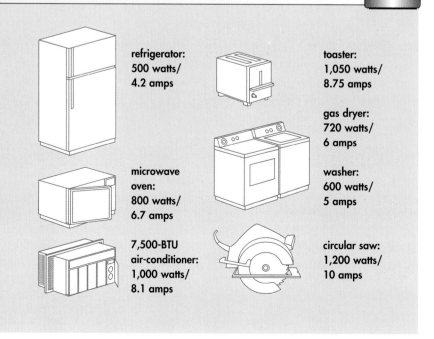

refrigerator:
500 watts/
4.2 amps

toaster:
1,050 watts/
8.75 amps

gas dryer:
720 watts/
6 amps

microwave
oven:
800 watts/
6.7 amps

washer:
600 watts/
5 amps

7,500-BTU
air-conditioner:
1,000 watts/
8.1 amps

circular saw:
1,200 watts/
10 amps

MAPPING YOUR CIRCUITS

When you look inside the door of your service panel, do you see a detailed description of what each branch circuit controls? If not, make a chart yourself. You'll be glad you mapped the circuits the next time you have to turn off a circuit for repairs or improvements.

Begin by making a map of each floor in the house. Take care to include all receptacles, switches, appliances, and fixtures. Be aware that 240-volt receptacles will have their own circuits. With a large house, you may have to make more than one drawing per floor.

Mapping is best done with a helper to flip switches and test outlets while you stay at the box and write down findings. If you must work alone, plug in a radio turned to peak volume to find the general area covered by the circuit. The radio will go silent when you switch off the current. Test outlets to find the extent of the circuit.

1. Test each outlet.
Mark each circuit breaker or fuse with a number. Turn on all the appliances and lights on one floor. Plug a lamp into every receptacle. Turn off one circuit, and have your helper write the circuit number next to each outlet that went dead.

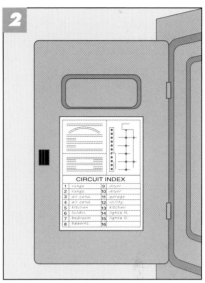

2. Make a record on the panel.
Continue the test with every circuit for every floor. Transfer the findings onto a sheet of paper you will affix to the inside of the circuit box door.

THE NEC

Electrical codes are based on the National Electrical Code (NEC), which is published by a non-profit organization and is upgraded periodically. The NEC code itself is a huge book that covers every conceivable electrical situation. It provides the model on which virtually all local codes are based.

Some communities simply adopt the code as their own; others modify it. Any time you want to make a change in your electrical service, check the NEC and local codes before you begin (see pages 4–5).

LOAD WORKSHEET		
circuit #5		
voltage 120		
circuit breaker amperage 20		
(20x.80=16 amps)		
CUSTOMER	WATTS ÷ VOLTAGE =	AMPERAGE
coffee pot	650 ÷ 120 =	5.42
fluorescent work lites		
	ballast amperage =	.66
toaster	1050 ÷ 120 =	8.75
	total exist. load	14.80
new exhaust fan		
	100 ÷ 120 =	.83
	new total load	15.63

3. Make a load sheet.
To really get a fix on how your house uses electricity, combine the information you have just gathered with the power-use information printed on appliances. Write up a load sheet, as shown. It will help you assess capacity for future additions to your electrical system.

ESSENTIAL TOOLS

You don't need to purchase an arsenal of specialized tools to do the electrical projects in this book. For most repairs, a minor outlay will be enough to equip you adequately.

Needle-nose and **lineman's pliers** are musts. You need the first to bend wires into the loops required for many electrical connections. Lineman's pliers make it possible to neatly twist wires together. Both also are used to cut wires. **Side-cutting pliers** make it easy to snip wires in tight places and are ideal for cutting sheathing off cable.

For stripping wires, use an **adjustable wire stripper** or a **combination tool,** which also crimps and cuts wire. If you're working with nonmetallic cable, use a **cable ripper** to remove the sheathing easily without nicking the wires. A simple **neon tester** will tell you if an outlet or fixture is live. A **beaded chain** simplifies fishing thin, low-voltage wires or phone wires through walls.

General carpentry tools that come in handy when doing electrical work include an **electric drill** with a **spade bit** to make holes for cable to pass through; a **utility knife, screwdrivers,** a **keyhole saw** for cutting drywall, a **level,** a **hacksaw** for cutting conduit and metal-sheathed cable, and a **tape measure.**

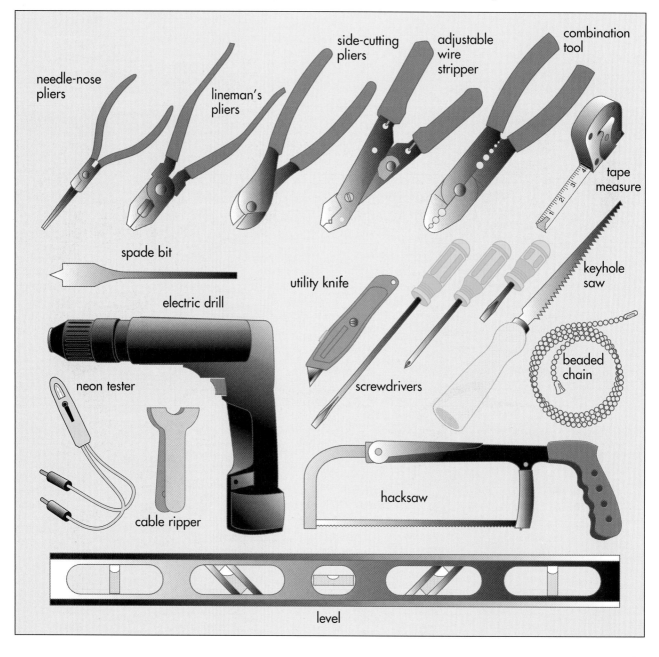

SPECIALIZED TOOLS

As you take on more complicated electrical projects, you will find that other tools are invaluable. Some of these tools are essential to such projects; others simply help you do a better, faster job.

If you need to drill holes deeper than the length of your spade bit, get a **bit extension.** A **soldering gun** with a spool of **lead-free, rosin-core solder** will be necessary if local codes require soldering. Don't pull a cartridge-type fuse by hand—always use a **fuse puller.** A **BX cutter** (this tool can be rented) makes easy and safe work of cutting metal-sheathed cable. A **tubing cutter** quickly makes clean cuts in conduit. When working with conduit, use a **conduit bender** to shape the material without crimping it and **tongue-and-groove pliers** for tightening connectors. For running cable through finished walls and ceilings or wire through conduit, a **fish tape** makes the job easier.

A **continuity tester** has a small bulb and battery for testing fuses, switches, and sockets with the power off. A **voltmeter** works with the power on or off and indicates the amount of voltage at an outlet. A **receptacle analyzer** runs a number of tests, telling you if your receptacle has a faulty connection and if it is properly grounded and polarized.

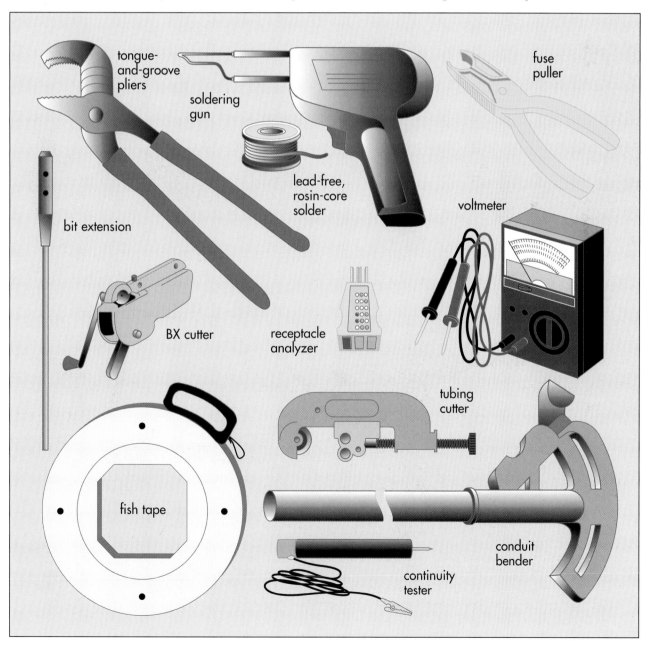

CHOOSING SWITCHES

Manufacturers offer a sometimes bewildering array of switches. To begin with, you have a choice of colors—brown, ivory, and white are the most readily available. But the differences extend far beyond appearance.

For most of your needs, you'll probably choose a **single-pole toggle,** which is available for a low price. "Toggle" simply refers to a switch that flips up and down.

Three-way and **four-way** switches are needed if you want to control a light from two or three separate switches. To learn about wiring them, see pages 87–90.

If you want to add a switch without putting in a larger box, a **double** switch may be the solution. It takes up the same amount of space as a single switch.

A **rocker** switch functions the same way as a standard toggle switch but is slightly easier to use.

A **dimmer** switch allows you to adjust lighting levels to suit your needs. A sliding dimmer brightens the light as you slide it upward. The rotary type comes in two versions. One version turns lights on or off with a push; the light level is altered by turning the knob. The other type dims the light as the knob is rotated counterclockwise until it turns off.

EXPERTS' INSIGHT

LOOK FOR THE UL SYMBOL
The UL symbol means that electrical materials have been checked for any defects by Underwriters Laboratories, an independent testing organization. Local codes may prohibit using items not UL-listed.

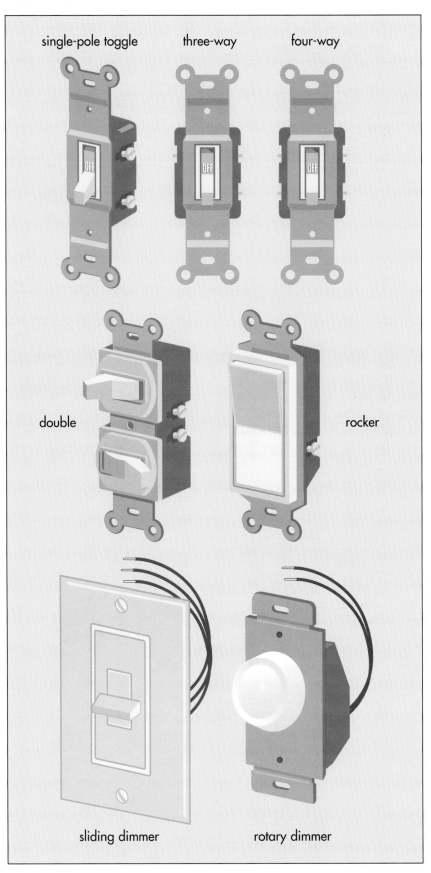

single-pole toggle three-way four-way

double rocker

sliding dimmer rotary dimmer

SELECTING SPECIALTY SWITCHES

Of the many available switches built to suit special needs, the ones on this page are some of the most common. Take a trip to a home center or a lighting store, and you may find the switch that does exactly what you want. To find out how to install these switches, see pages 74–75.

If you have power tools or other devices that you don't want children to play with, consider installing a **tamperproof** switch. Operated only with a key, it can be wired to control the receptacle to which such items are connected.

For security in your backyard, or to have a light automatically greet you as you approach your house, choose a **motion-sensor security** switch. Its wide-angle infrared beam detects motion and turns the light on automatically. With most units, you can choose how long the light will stay on.

A **pilot-light** switch has a little bulb that glows when power is flowing through the switch. Use it when a fixture or appliance is out of sight. Closet lights, attic exhaust fans, basement lights, and garage lights often are controlled by pilot-light switches.

If you need to squeeze both a switch and an outlet into a single box, use a **switch/receptacle.** Also use this switch to easily add a receptacle to a room. This switch can be wired so the receptacle is live all the time or wired so the switch controls the receptacle.

A **programmable** switch comes with digital controls and can be programmed to turn lights on and off up to four times a day. This type of switch is useful for security and deterring burglars when you are away from home.

A **time-delay** switch has a dial that can be set to leave a fixture running for up to 60 minutes. Use one for a vent fan, space heater, heat lamp, or garage light.

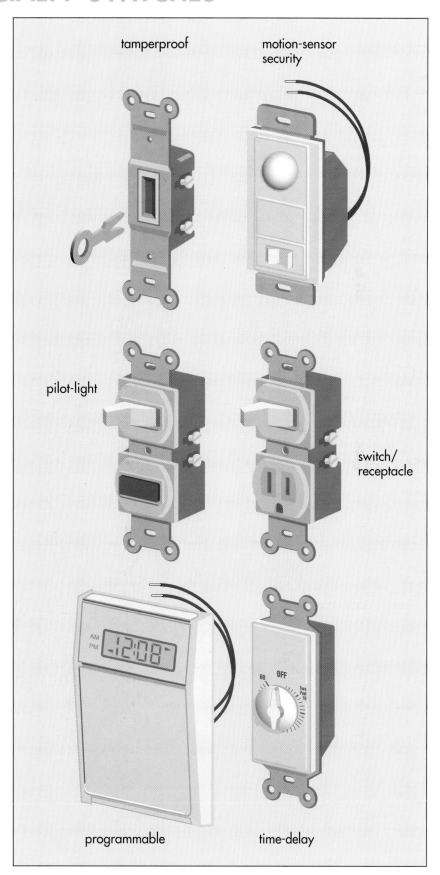

tamperproof

motion-sensor security

pilot-light

switch/ receptacle

programmable

time-delay

CHOOSING RECEPTACLES

A standard duplex receptacle has two outlets for receiving plugs. Each outlet has a long (neutral) slot, a shorter (hot) slot, and a half-round grounding hole. This ensures that the plug will be polarized and grounded (see page 10). Receptacles are rated for maximum amps. A **20-amp grounded receptacle** has a T-shaped neutral slot; use it only on 20-amp circuits. For most purposes, a **15-amp grounded receptacle** is sufficient. When replacing a receptacle in an ungrounded outlet box, use a **15-amp ungrounded receptacle,** intended only for use in older homes without ground wires in the circuits. Use a three-pronged plug adapter on an ungrounded receptacle only if the wall-plate screw is grounded (see page 59 to test this). The switch in a combination **switch/receptacle** can be hooked up to control the receptacle it's paired with. A **20-amp single grounded receptacle** makes it nearly impossible to overload a critical circuit. For outdoors, in basements, or within 6 feet of a water fixture, install **ground-fault circuit-interrupter (GFCI)** receptacles (see page 77). Select a **240-volt receptacle** based on the appliance amperage rating. Plugs required for appliances of 15, 20, 30, and 50 amps will have different prong configurations.

> ### CAUTION!
> *REPLACE, DON'T CHANGE*
> *Replace a receptacle with one that is just like the old one. Change types only if you are certain that the wiring is suitable. Do not replace an ungrounded outlet with a grounded one unless you know the box is grounded.*

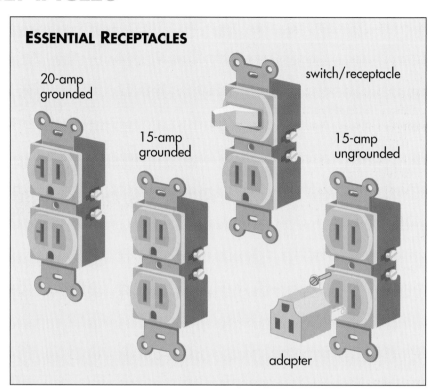

ESSENTIAL RECEPTACLES

20-amp grounded

15-amp grounded

switch/receptacle

15-amp ungrounded

adapter

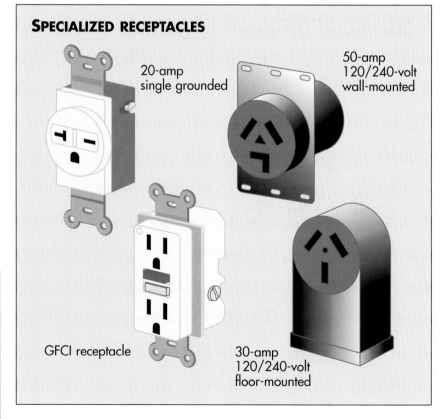

SPECIALIZED RECEPTACLES

20-amp single grounded

50-amp 120/240-volt wall-mounted

GFCI receptacle

30-amp 120/240-volt floor-mounted

CHOOSING WIRE AND CABLE

Wire, cord, and cable (generically referred to as "conductors") are the pathways along which electricity travels. Wire is a solid strand of metal encased in insulation. Cord is a group of small strands encased in insulation. Cable is made of two or more wires wrapped in protective sheathing of metal or plastic.

Most local codes allow you to use nonmetallic sheathed cable (NM cable) inside walls, floors, and other places where it can't be damaged and won't get wet. Information printed on the sheathing tells you what is inside. The top example at right has two 14-gauge wires plus a bare ground wire, and is thus referred to as "14-2 G" cable ("G" for ground). Cable marked "14-3" has three wires plus a ground wire. Flexible armored cable (BX) contains wires wrapped in a flexible metal sheathing. It can be used for short runs in exposed areas such as attics or basements. BX needs no separate ground wire because the metal sheathing itself conducts the ground. Underground feed (UF) cable is watertight, with the sheathing molded around the wire. Many municipalities permit this for underground lines.

Different gauge wires carry different amounts of electricity— 14-gauge carries a maximum of 15 amps, 12-gauge carries up to 20 amps, and 10-gauge wire up to 30 amps. Unsheathed wires are pulled through flexible or rigid conduit. Flexible metal conduit, or Greenfield, looks like armored cable but doesn't contain wires. It is cut to length, wires are pulled through it, and the completed pieces installed (see pages 40–41). With conduit, you pull wires through it after it's installed (see pages 42–45). Doorbells and other low-voltage circuits typically use 18-gauge wire.

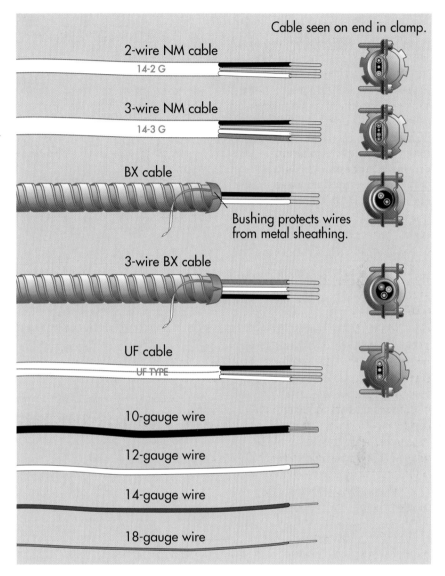

Cable seen on end in clamp.

2-wire NM cable
14-2 G

3-wire NM cable
14-3 G

BX cable
Bushing protects wires from metal sheathing.

3-wire BX cable

UF cable
UF TYPE

10-gauge wire

12-gauge wire

14-gauge wire

18-gauge wire

WHAT THE COLORS MEAN	
Color	**Function**
white	neutral, carrying power back to the service panel
black	hot, carrying power from the service panel
red and other colors	also hot, color-coded to help identify which circuit they are on
white with black tape	a white wire that is being used as a hot wire
bare or green	a ground wire

CHOOSING BOXES

An electrical box has one primary function—to house electrical connections. Those connections might be to a switch, a receptacle, the leads of a light fixture, or other sets of wires.

Electrical codes require that all wire connections or cable splices be inside an approved metal or plastic box. And every box must be accessible—you cannot bury it inside a wall. This protects your home from the danger of fire and makes it easier to inspect and upgrade your wiring in the future.

Codes govern how many connections you're allowed to make within a box, depending on its size. If you must make more connections, you have to use a larger box (see chart at right).

There are boxes to suit most any depth of wall or ceiling, boxes to support heavy fixtures such as ceiling fans, and boxes for remodeling work and new construction. If, for instance, you'll be pulling cables through a finished wall, you can choose from a number of retrofit boxes that can be mounted with a minimum of damage to the wall.

Boxes for switches and receptacles serve as the workhorses in any electrical installation. Some of the metal ones can be "ganged" into double, triple, or larger multiples by removing one side and linking them together. Switch/receptacle boxes made of plastic are accepted by most codes, but they can't be ganged. If you are using conduit, Greenfield, or BX, you must use metal boxes to ground the system.

Utility boxes are surface-mounted in basements and garages to hold switches or receptacles. Boxes for fixtures or junctions may support lighting fixtures or split circuits into separate branches.

MEASUREMENTS
CHOOSING THE CORRECT BOX SIZE

Type of Box	Size in Inches (Height × Width × Depth)	Maximum Number of Wires Allowed in a Box		
		14-gauge	12-gauge	10-gauge
switch/ receptacle	3×2×1½	3	3	3
	3×2×2	5	4	4
	3×2×2¼	5	4	4
	3×2×2½	6	5	5
	3×2×2¾	7	6	5
	3×2×3½	9	8	7
utility	4×2⅛×1½	5	4	4
	4×2⅛×1⅞	6	5	5
	4×2⅛×2⅛	7	6	5
fixture/ junction	4×1¼ round or octagonal	6	5	5
	4×1½ round or octagonal	7	6	6
	4×2⅛ round or octagonal	10	9	8
	4×1¼ square	9	8	7
	4×1½ square	10	9	8
	4×2⅛ square	15	13	12
	4¹¹⁄₁₆×1½ square	14	13	11
	4¹¹⁄₁₆×2⅛ square	21	18	16

EXPERTS' INSIGHT

BOX CAPACITY

Overcrowd a box and you risk damaging wire connectors, piercing insulation, and cracking a switch or receptacle, any of which could cause a short. That is why codes spell out how many wires you can install in a box.

The chart above gives standard requirements. Other items may add to the total number of wires a box can hold. As you count wires, keep in mind these rules:

■ Don't count fixture leads (the wires that are connected to the fixture).

■ Count a wire that enters and leaves without a splice as one.

■ Count each type of cable clamp, stud, or hickey inside the box as one wire.

■ Count each receptacle or switch as two.

■ Count grounding wires entering a box as one, but do not count grounding wires that begin and end in the box.

NEW INSTALLATION SWITCH/RECEPTACLE BOXES

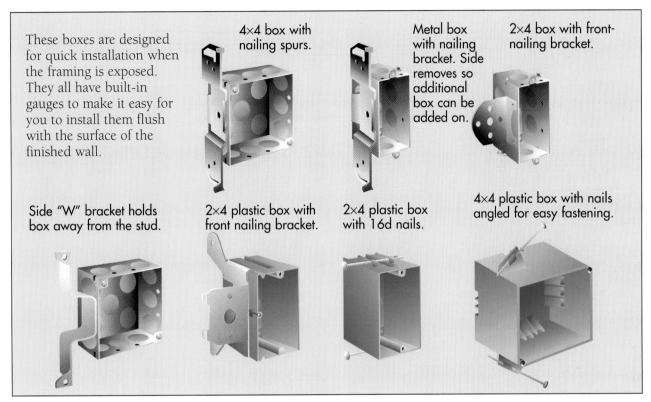

These boxes are designed for quick installation when the framing is exposed. They all have built-in gauges to make it easy for you to install them flush with the surface of the finished wall.

4×4 box with nailing spurs.

Metal box with nailing bracket. Side removes so additional box can be added on.

2×4 box with front-nailing bracket.

Side "W" bracket holds box away from the stud.

2×4 plastic box with front nailing bracket.

2×4 plastic box with 16d nails.

4×4 plastic box with nails angled for easy fastening.

RETROFIT SWITCH/RECEPTACLE BOXES

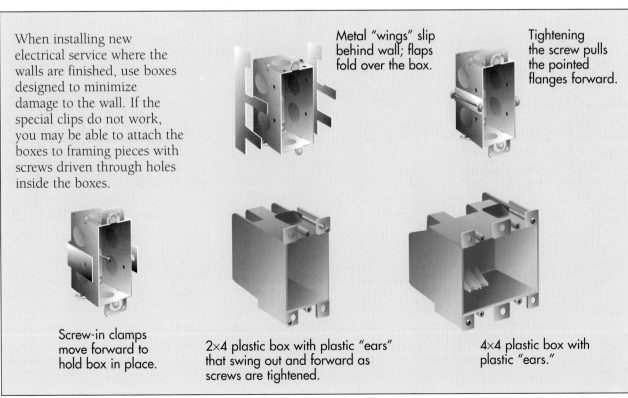

When installing new electrical service where the walls are finished, use boxes designed to minimize damage to the wall. If the special clips do not work, you may be able to attach the boxes to framing pieces with screws driven through holes inside the boxes.

Metal "wings" slip behind wall; flaps fold over the box.

Tightening the screw pulls the pointed flanges forward.

Screw-in clamps move forward to hold box in place.

2×4 plastic box with plastic "ears" that swing out and forward as screws are tightened.

4×4 plastic box with plastic "ears."

NEW INSTALLATION FIXTURE/JUNCTION BOXES

"New installation" wiring refers to work done on a freshly framed wall. With no drywall or plaster in the way, it is easy to install ceiling fixture boxes that are solid enough to hold a heavy chandelier or a fan. Remember that all junction boxes must remain accessible— never cover them with drywall.

Telescoping brackets allow you to position these boxes anywhere between joists.

Metal octagonal box requires framing behind it if it is to support a heavy fixture.

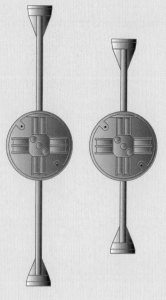

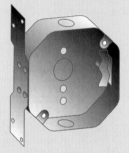

Round plastic fixture box has a bracket with sharp points so you can quickly tap it in place then secure it with screws.

Octagonal junction box with side bracket is nailed to framing.

RETROFIT FIXTURE/JUNCTION BOXES

The retrofitting of adding new wiring to old walls is challenging. Often it's not easy to secure a fixture box when there's drywall or plaster in the way. For heavy ceiling fixtures, use a brace bar that can be slipped into the hole and expanded from joist to joist (see page 81).

A shallow box like this is sometimes needed in older homes with plaster walls.

"Wings" come forward as you tighten their screws, clasping the box to the plaster or drywall.

Most retrofitting starts with standard junction boxes located in accessible areas.

EXPERTS' INSIGHT

USE NEW INSTALLATION BOXES IN UNFINISHED SPACES

Most homes have areas where the walls or ceilings are unfinished, such as basements, attics, and garages. Whenever you are adding improvements to these areas, or adding junction boxes that will serve existing circuits, use new installation boxes. Use metal boxes with metal cover plates, even if you are using nonmetallic sheathed cable, because they may get bumped. Plastic boxes will crack.

SPECIALIZED BOXES

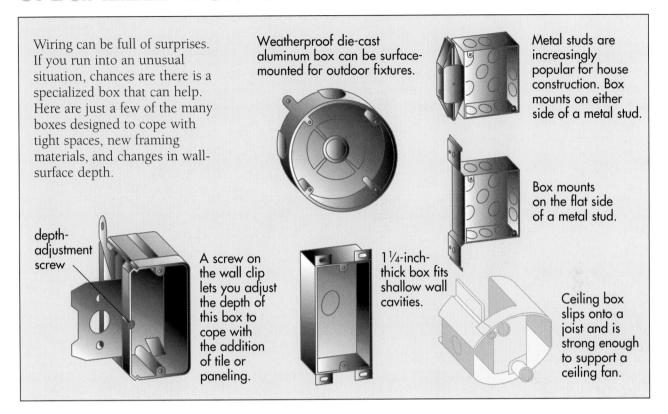

Wiring can be full of surprises. If you run into an unusual situation, chances are there is a specialized box that can help. Here are just a few of the many boxes designed to cope with tight spaces, new framing materials, and changes in wall-surface depth.

Weatherproof die-cast aluminum box can be surface-mounted for outdoor fixtures.

Metal studs are increasingly popular for house construction. Box mounts on either side of a metal stud.

Box mounts on the flat side of a metal stud.

depth-adjustment screw

A screw on the wall clip lets you adjust the depth of this box to cope with the addition of tile or paneling.

1¼-inch-thick box fits shallow wall cavities.

Ceiling box slips onto a joist and is strong enough to support a ceiling fan.

BOX ACCESSORIES

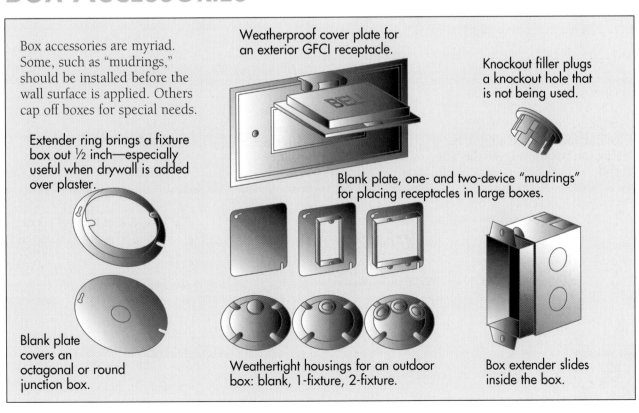

Box accessories are myriad. Some, such as "mudrings," should be installed before the wall surface is applied. Others cap off boxes for special needs.

Weatherproof cover plate for an exterior GFCI receptacle.

Knockout filler plugs a knockout hole that is not being used.

Extender ring brings a fixture box out ½ inch—especially useful when drywall is added over plaster.

Blank plate, one- and two-device "mudrings" for placing receptacles in large boxes.

Blank plate covers an octagonal or round junction box.

Weathertight housings for an outdoor box: blank, 1-fixture, 2-fixture.

Box extender slides inside the box.

INSTALLING BOXES IN UNFINISHED SPACE

To wire a room with unfinished walls, such as a basement remodeling or a room addition, you'll need boxes fastened to the framing. When attaching the boxes, be sure they protrude from the framing the same thickness as your drywall or paneling—usually ½ inch. Run cable from box to box and to the service panel.

After you've roughed in the wiring, but before you install the switches and receptacles, put up the drywall on the walls and ceiling. Finish and prime the surfaces, and install the devices in the boxes.

YOU'LL NEED...

TIME: About 3 hours for installing 10 boxes.
SKILLS: Basic carpentry skills.
TOOLS: Tape measure, hammer or drill with screwdriver bit.

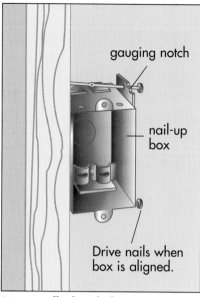

Nonmetallic handy box
Many boxes have a series of gauging notches on their sides. Determine the thickness of the drywall and/or paneling you will be installing, and align the box to the appropriate notch as you attach it. A nail-up box like this one is the easiest to install.

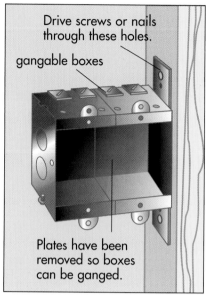

Gangable boxes
These have detachable sides, so you can attach them together to form double- or triple-size boxes. To attach such boxes without special mounting hardware, simply drive screws or nails through the holes and into the framing.

MEASUREMENTS

PLACING BOXES
In a typical room, place switch boxes 48–50 inches above the floor and receptacles 12–16 inches above floor level. Check with local codes to see how many receptacles you will need. In most cases they must be placed so that no point along any wall is more than 6 feet from a receptacle. This means that you'll have to install at least one receptacle every 12 feet along the wall. For kitchens and bathrooms, special requirements apply.

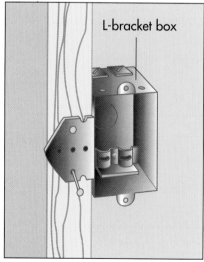

L-bracket box
Some L-bracket boxes adjust to suit the thickness of your wall material. Others accommodate only one thickness. Hold the box in position against the framing, and drive two nails or screws through the holes in the bracket.

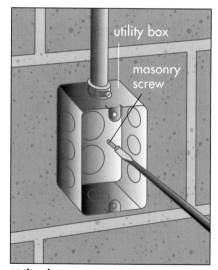

Utility box
Use a utility box and conduit or armored cable in an area where you don't need a finished appearance. If you're attaching boxes to masonry, use anchors or masonry screws.

*F*ixture and junction boxes are easy to install in unfinished space. Install boxes so they will be flush with the finished surface of the ceiling or wall. Do not place any electrical box where it will be covered by drywall or paneling.

If there is a joist at the spot where you want the box, use a box with a **hanger bracket** or an **L-bracket.** This page shows various types available—some designed for working from below, some for working from above. These fasten to the joist with screws or nails. When fastening, allow for the thickness of the ceiling material.

If you need to install a fixture box between joists, use a box with a **bar hanger.** Attach the ends of the brackets to the joists, and slide the box into the desired position.

Junction boxes protect wire connections or cable splices. Some junction boxes come with brackets. Others just nail or screw to a joist, stud, or rafter.

Regardless of the type of box you're installing, always secure it with two fasteners. If the box will be supporting a ceiling fan or other heavy fixture, make sure it's anchored securely enough to carry the load. If a box has been correctly mounted but still doesn't feel firm enough, add a framing piece and secure it to that as well.

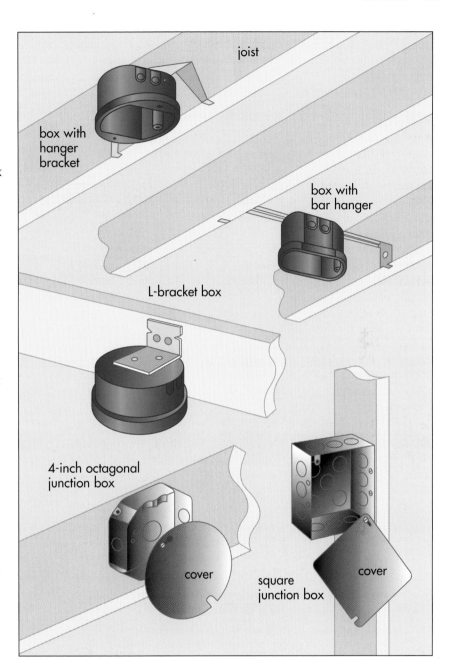

joist

box with hanger bracket

box with bar hanger

L-bracket box

4-inch octagonal junction box

cover

square junction box

cover

OVERHEAD LIGHT PLACEMENT

■ One pleasing way to light a room is with recessed can lights (see pages 70–71) or small fixtures. To plan for a group of symmetrically placed lights, make a map of your ceiling and experiment by drawing circles, each of which represents the area lit up by a recessed fixture.

■ When you experiment with your design, try to arrange the lights so they are half as far from the walls as they are from each other. A pleasingly symmetrical pattern usually results. Start by arranging lights 6 feet apart and 3 feet from walls. Avoid positioning them closer than 4 feet apart. Add to your plan any suspended or track lighting you need for task illumination or to accent an attractive area of the room.

■ Don't expect to achieve an arrangement that's perfectly symmetrical; few ceilings will allow for that. Also keep in mind that with recessed lighting, you may not be able to put all the lights exactly where you want them, because there will be joists in the way (see page 70). In most cases, a less-than-perfect arrangement will not be noticeable.

INSTALLING BOXES IN FINISHED SPACE

Installing electrical work is a greater challenge when the walls and ceilings are finished. Often, patching and painting can take far more time than the electrical work itself! Plan the placement so you avoid making unnecessary holes.

Wherever possible, avoid making contact with the framing. Using special boxes designed for installation in finished space, you often can simply make a hole the size of the box and secure the box to the wall or ceiling surface.

Before you begin, plan how you're going to get cable to the new location (see pages 32–35).

YOU'LL NEED...
TIME: About 30 minutes a box, not including running new wire.
SKILLS: Simple skills are required.
TOOLS: Keyhole saw, screwdriver, needle-nose pliers, utility knife, and neon tester.

1. Determine box location.
Drill a small hole in the wall. Insert a bent wire and rotate it. If you hit something, you've probably found a stud. Try 6 inches to one side. If you strike wood again, you may have hit a fire block. Drill another hole 3 inches higher or lower. Keep trying until you can rotate the bent wire freely.

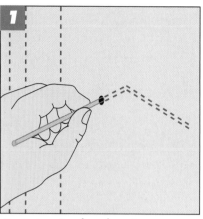

2. Trace around box.
Some boxes come with a template that can be held against the surface and traced around. Otherwise, use the box itself and center it on the hole you could rotate the wire in. Make sure the template or box is plumb before you mark the outline.

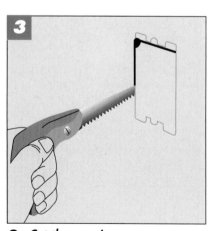

3. Cut the opening.
Carefully cut around the traced outline. If the surface is drywall, use a utility knife. If you are cutting into plaster walls, use a keyhole saw. If the plaster is crumbly, mask the outline with tape. For a wood-surfaced wall, drill a ¼-inch access hole in each corner and use a saber saw. Run cable (see pages 32–35).

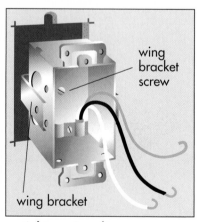

4. Fasten with side clamps ...
Side-clamp boxes grip the wall from behind when you tighten the screws. Pull 8 inches of cable through the box and insert the box. Hold the box plumb as you tighten the clamps. Alternate from side to side as you work so the box seats evenly. Avoid overtightening the clamps.

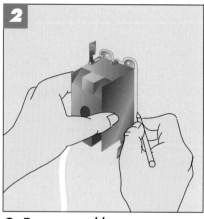

wing bracket screw

wing bracket

or tighten wing clips.
Loosen the screw centered in the receptacle box until the wing bracket is at maximum extension from the back. Hold the wings against the body of the box and push the box into the hole. Tighten the screw until the box is held firmly in place.

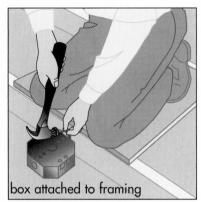

box attached to framing

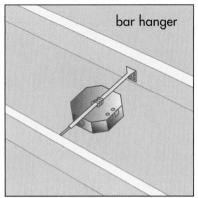

bar hanger

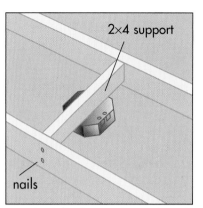

2×4 support

nails

With access from above

A ceiling box must support a fixture, so it must to be securely attached to the framing. If you are fortunate enough to have

attic space above, the job can be done without damaging your ceiling. Mark the location of each box on the ceiling, and drive nails as reference points.

Cut the hole for the box. If there is a nearby joist, attach an L-bracket box directly to it. If not, use a bar hanger, or frame in a 2×4 support.

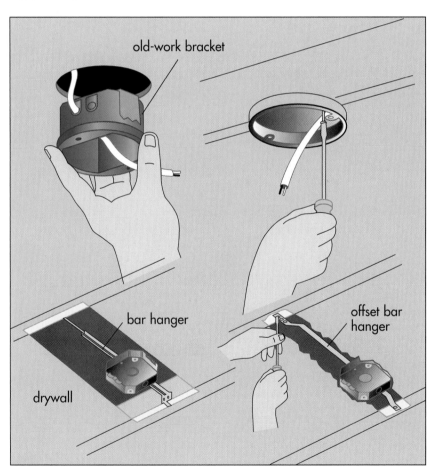

old-work bracket

bar hanger

drywall

offset bar hanger

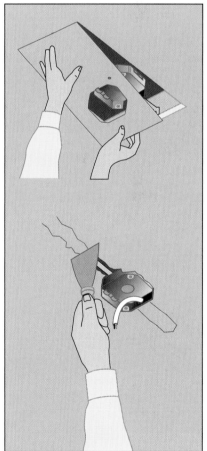

With no access from above

If you cannot work from above, use one of these methods. For most light fixtures, which weigh less than 5 pounds, use an old-work bracket. Cut the hole the size of the box, slip the bracket in, telescope it to fit between two joists, and attach the box to it.

For heavier fixtures, such as chandeliers and ceiling fans, make an opening in the ceiling and install hanging hardware. With a drywall ceiling, cut out a large rectangle and install a bar hanger. With plaster, chip out a path and use an offset bar hanger.

Repair the ceiling.

After checking the electrical installation, patch the ceiling. With drywall, you may be able to use the same piece you cut out. Nail the panel to the joists, and tape the seam with joint compound. For a plaster ceiling, fill with patching compound.

STRIPPING WIRE

Before making electrical connections, you'll need to remove some of the sheathing that encases the three or four wires of the cable, and strip some of the insulation that coats the individual wires. Stripping techniques are simple, but exercise care when removing sheathing in order to avoid damaging any of the underlying insulation. Also, be careful to strip the insulation without nicking the copper wire—this would weaken it.

Instead of stripping the wires after the cable is pulled into the box, strip wires before inserting them. That way, if you make a mistake, you can cut off the damaged portion and try again.

YOU'LL NEED...
TIME: About 5 minutes or less.
SKILLS: Simple stripping.
TOOLS: Cable ripper, utility knife, side cutters.

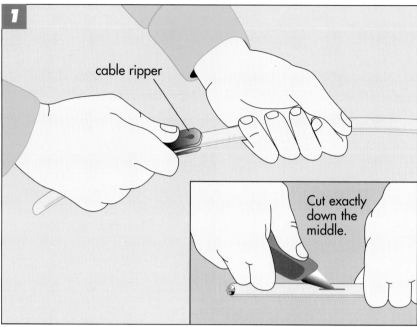

1. Slit the sheathing.
The easiest way to remove plastic sheathing from nonmetallic sheathed cable is to use an inexpensive cable ripper. Slip 6 to 8 inches of cable into the ripper's jaws, squeeze, and pull. This slits open the sheathing without damaging the insulation of internal wires. The same job can be done with a knife, but you must be careful: Run the blade right down the middle so it doesn't strip insulation from the wires.

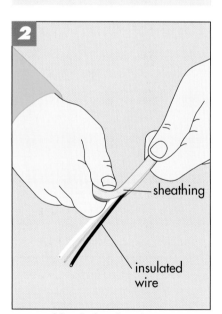

2. Peel back the sheathing.
Pull back the sheathing you have just slit, as well as the paper wrapping or strips of thin plastic, if any. You'll find two or three separately insulated wires, as well as a bare ground wire.

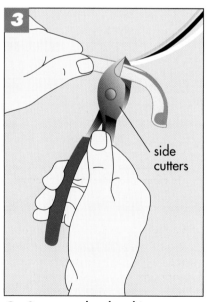

3. Cut away the sheathing.
Cut off the sheathing and paper. Remove the slit sheathing with a pair of side cutters. Or use a knife, taking care to point the blade away from the wires.

CAUTION!
This job is simple, but it must be done with great care, or you could end up with dangerous electrical shorts. If you think you may have accidentally damaged some insulation, cut the cable back to a place behind the potentially dangerous spot, and start again.
Another possible problem: If you cut into the copper wire while stripping the insulation, you can weaken the wire, so that it is liable to break while you are making a connection later.

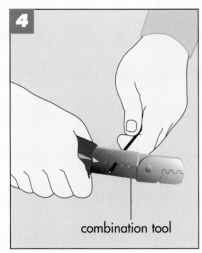

combination tool

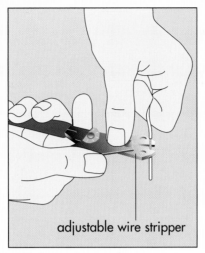

adjustable wire stripper

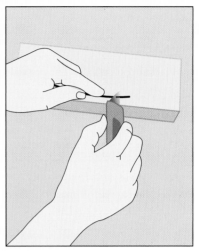

4. Strip the wire.

To strip insulation from wires, use a combination tool, which has separate holes for the different sizes of wires. Locate the wire in the correct hole, clamp down, give it a twist, and

pull the tool away from you. Use the same technique with an adjustable stripper. The advantage of this tool is that, once it is set correctly for the wire size, it is not necessary to look for the right hole every

time. Stripping also can be done with a utility knife, but be careful not to dig into the copper wire. Place the wire on a scrap piece of wood, hold the blade at a slight angle, and make several light slices.

JOINING WIRES

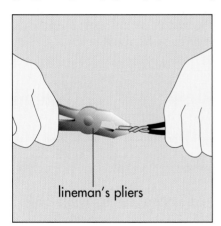

lineman's pliers

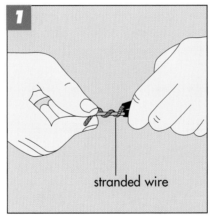

stranded wire

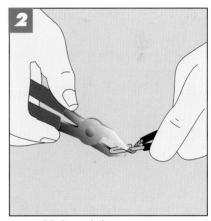

Joining solid wires

Join solid wires by using a pair of lineman's pliers. Cross the two wires, grab both wires with the pliers, and twist clockwise. Both wires should twist—do not just twist one wire around the other. Twist for several revolutions, but don't twist so tightly that the wires are in danger of breaking. Screw a wire connector onto the two wires (see page 30).

1. Joining stranded to solid wires

Often, a stranded wire (made of many thin wires) has to be spliced to a solid wire, as when hooking up a light fixture or dimmer switch. Because the stranded wire is more flexible, the two won't twist together. Wrap the stranded wire around the solid wire.

2. Fold the solid wire over.

Bend the solid wire so it clamps down on the stranded wire. Screw a wire connector onto the two wires (see page 30), and wrap the connection with electrician's tape.

WORKING WITH WIRE

The final—and most gratifying—phase of an electrical installation comes when you tie all those wires together and attach them to the switches, light fixtures, and receptacles. Don't take shortcuts with wire connections and splices. Cap splices with wire connectors rather than only tape, and wrap tape around each connector. Make pigtails (see page 31) wherever they are needed instead of trying to connect two or more wires to a terminal. Finally, don't overcrowd a box with too many wires (for limits, see chart on page 20).

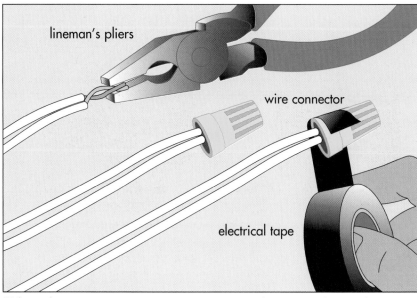

HOW MANY WIRES IN A CONNECTOR?

Wire connector	12-gauge wires	14-gauge wires
red	2–4	2–5
yellow	2–3	2–4
orange	2	2–4

Using wire connectors

To complete a splice of two or more wires, use wire connectors. These come in a variety of sizes. Select the size you need depending on how many wires you will connect as well as the thickness of the wires (see chart, left). Wire connectors firm up the splice and protect bare wires better than tape. First twist the wires firmly together. Do not depend on the connector to do the joining. Twist the wire connector on, turning it by hand until it tightens firmly. As a final precaution, wrap the connector clockwise with electrical tape, overlapping the wires.

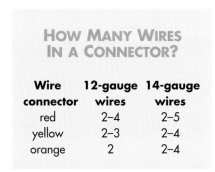

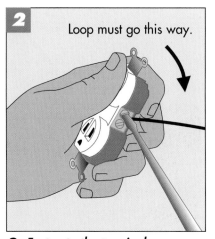

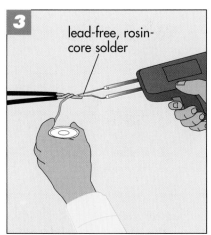

1. To connect a wire to a terminal, form a loop.

Strip just enough wire to wrap around the terminal—about ¾ inch. Then form it into a loop using needle-nose or lineman's pliers. It takes practice to make loops that lie flat and are neither too big nor too small.

2. Fasten to the terminal.

Hook the wire clockwise around the terminal so that tightening the screw will close the loop. With receptacles, the black wires go to the brass side, white to silver. Tighten firmly, but avoid overtightening, which can damage the device. If you do crack a device in any way, throw it out.

3. Solder a splice.

A few codes require that splices be soldered. More often, soldering house wiring is prohibited. If you need to solder a splice, start by twisting the wires together. Heat the wires with a soldering iron, then touch lead-free, rosin-core solder to the splice. The solder should melt into the splice.

CONNECTING WIRES

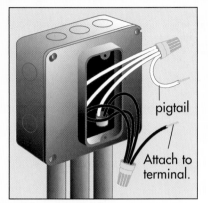

Add a pigtail where two or more wires attach to a terminal ...

Never attach more than one wire to a terminal. Codes prohibit it, and it's unsafe because terminal screws are made to hold only one wire. An easier way to join many wires to a terminal is to cut a short piece of wire (about 4 inches), strip both ends, and splice it to the other wires as shown to form a pigtail.

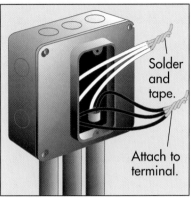

or make a soldered splice.

Twist wires together so that one extends 1 inch beyond the splice. Solder the twist and loop the extended wire. Tape the soldered splice before screwing the wire to the terminal.

CAUTION!
Make sure local codes permit soldering.

CAUTION!
Most receptacles and switches have connection holes in the back. To make a connection, strip the wire (a stripping gauge often is provided, showing you how much insulation to remove) and poke it into the correct hole. On a receptacle, the holes are marked for white and black wires. However, most professionals do not use these holes. Wires inserted this way are simply not as secure as those screwed to a terminal.

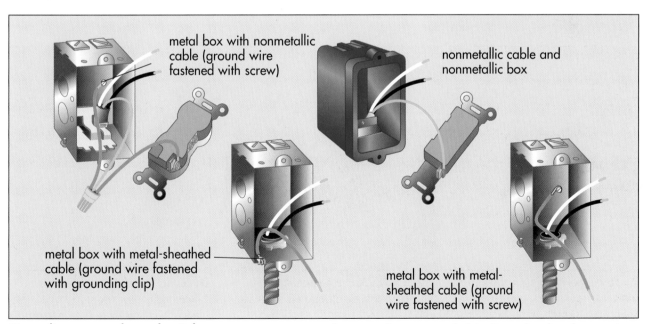

Grounding receptacles and switches

How you ground receptacles and switches depends on the type of wiring you're using as well as the type of box. With flexible armored cable (BX), Greenfield, or rigid conduit, the metal of the wiring casing and the metal of the box substitutes for the grounding wire. Simply by attaching the device firmly to the box, you have grounded it. Some local codes require that you also attach a short grounding wire, as shown. If you're working with nonmetallic sheathed cable (Romex) and metal boxes, connect short grounding wires to the box and to the device. With nonmetallic boxes, the cable's grounding wire connects directly to the device.

RUNNING CABLE IN FINISHED SPACE

Do some detective work before running cable through finished walls and ceilings. As far as possible, determine what's in the wall or ceiling cavity. Look for access from an unfinished attic floor or basement ceiling. Check to see if there is insulation or blocking in the way. Determine whether or not there is a way to run cable parallel to the joists and studs. **TIP:** *Make as few holes as possible—often the most time-consuming part of running cable is patching walls and ceilings.* Use patching plaster, drywall tape, and compound to patch any holes.

YOU'LL NEED...

TIME: About 3 hours.
SKILLS: Drilling and patching.
TOOLS: Power drill, ¾- and 1-inch bits, fish tape, keyhole saw, utility knife, chisel, hammer, standard carpentry tools.

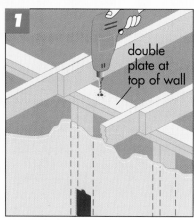

1. Drill top or bottom plates ...
If there is access from above or below, drill into the top or bottom plates of the wall frame. For a double plate or awkward angle, use a bit extension. After drilling the hole, feed the cable to the box opening. If you hit blocking (horizontal pieces between the studs), see Step 4.

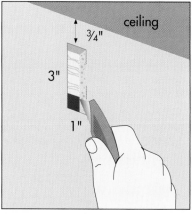

or cut an opening.
When there is no room for drilling through the plates from above or below, bore from the side instead. At the top of the wall, cut an opening to expose the single or double plate. At the bottom, there will only be a single plate; remove the baseboard, and make the cutout ¾ inch above the floor.

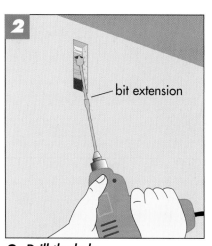

2. Drill the hole.
Using a bit extension, bore into the bottom of the plate, angling toward the center.

CAUTION!

Bore slowly to avoid burning out the drill. Watch out for nails. Wear goggles when working with power tools.

3. Push the cable through.
Push the cable up or down to the box opening. Then loop it through the plate. Pulling cable through walls is a two-person job. One person tugs—not too hard or the sheathing might tear—from the attic or basement. The other coils cable and feeds it through the opening, taking care to avoid kinks and knots.

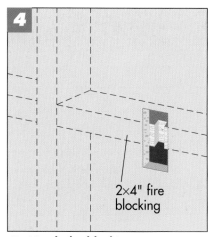

4. Notch the blocking.
To locate fire blocking, slip a tape measure through the hole and push it until it strikes the blocking. Measure to that point and make an opening that straddles the blocking. Chisel a notch that is large enough to accommodate the cable easily. After you've run the cable, but before you patch the hole, install a nail plate (see page 36).

Short runs of cable

Often it is easiest to fish cable from a nearby outlet. Before tapping into an outlet, make sure you won't be overloading the circuit (see pages 102–105). **NOTE:** *Shut off the power, remove the cover plate, and see if the receptacle has a set of unused terminals. If it doesn't, add pigtails (see page 31) before reconnecting.*

YOU'LL NEED...

TIME: About 2 hours, not including wall patching.
SKILLS: Pulling wire and patching drywall or plaster.
TOOLS: Fish tape, keyhole saw, standard carpentry tools.

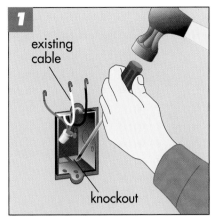

1. Open the box.
Disconnect the receptacle. Check for a cable clamp or other device that will attach the new cable to the box. If necessary, remove a knockout with a hammer and screwdriver and install a clamp.

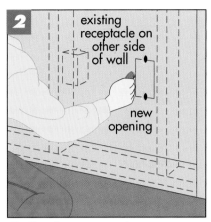

2. Cut the new opening.
Use a box as a template to mark the new outlet opening, and cut it open with a utility knife or keyhole saw. If possible, locate the new box in the same wall cavity as the source box.

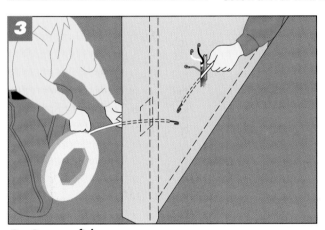

3. Connect fish tapes.
Thread one fish tape (or bent coat hanger) through the knockout hole, and another through the new opening. Wiggle one or both until they hook.

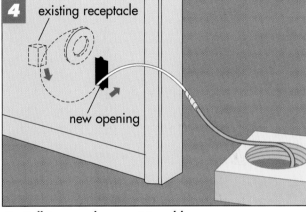

4. Pull tape and connect to cable.
Pull the tape from the existing box through the new opening. Strip some sheathing from the cable, hook the wires on the fish tape end, and wrap with tape.

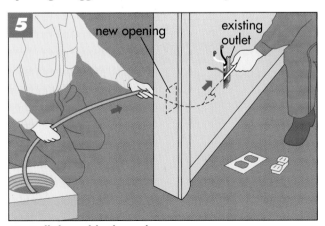

5. Pull the cable through.
Finally, pull the cable through the new opening and into the old box. Connect the cable to the old box (see page 39) and install the new box (see page 26).

CUT NOTCHES

To run cable past studs, cut openings that span each of the studs. Save the cutouts. Chisel a notch in the stud. Install a nail plate to protect the cable (see page 36) and patch the wall.

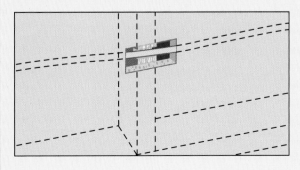

RUNNING CABLE ALONG BASEBOARDS

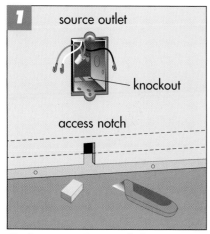

1 source outlet · knockout · access notch

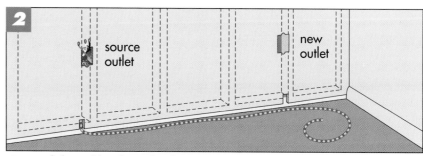

2 source outlet · new outlet

1. Remove trim, notch for access.
After cutting the hole for your new outlet, remove trim. Avoid damaging the wall or cracking the trim. Pop nails loose one at a time, levering the wood away from the wall with a pry bar. Once the board is free, make a notch in the wall below the outlet that will be the power source. If possible, cut the notch so the baseboard covers it when you replace the baseboard.

YOU'LL NEED...
TIME: 2 hours.
SKILLS: Cutting holes in walls, fishing cable, simple carpentry.
TOOLS: Utility knife, keyhole saw, chisel, standard carpentry tools.

EXPERTS' INSIGHT

Use armored flexible cable
Use only armored flexible cable (BX) for this operation—never nonmetallic sheathed cable, which can be easily pierced with a nail. Plan the location of the cable and the location of the nails so there is no danger of hitting the cable with a nail. Be especially careful when renailing baseboard, casing, and trim.

2. Feed the cable along the floor.
If your home has drywall, you may find a gap at the wall's base that's large enough to accommodate the cable. If there's no gap, cut a channel in the drywall for it. Feed the cable through a knockout hole in the source box, and pull it out of the wall below. As you run the cable along the floor, be sure that it is set back from the wall surface.

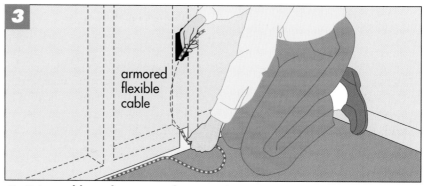

3 armored flexible cable

3. Bring cable to the new outlet.
If the new opening is low enough, simply push the cable up through the wall to the opening. To pull the cable up to a higher opening, use a fish tape (see page 33).

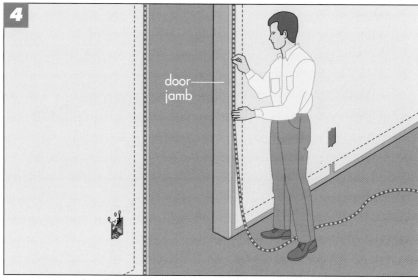

4 door jamb

4. Go around a door.
Carefully remove the casing from one side of the door jamb. Push the cable into the space between the jamb and the wall material, notching where necessary. When replacing the casing, be careful not to pierce the cable with the casing's nails.

RUNNING CABLE FOR CEILING FIXTURES

To run cable for a switch-controlled ceiling fixture, first determine the location and direction of the wall studs and ceiling joists. If possible, run wires parallel with framing members to save time-consuming work patching and painting. When cutting notches in drywall, make clean cuts and save the cutout pieces, if possible. Later, glue them back in place with construction adhesive, and finish with drywall tape and compound. Notches in plaster will require more work to repair. Fill the void with nonshrinking patching plaster.

YOU'LL NEED...

TIME: With a helper, 3 hours.
SKILLS: Cutting clean holes in walls, fishing cable.
TOOLS: Utility knife, keyhole saw, chisel, fish tape.

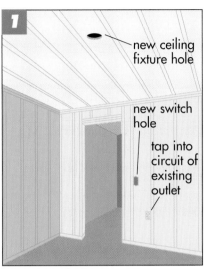

1. Cut the holes.
Decide where to locate the fixture. If a framing member is in the way, move the location of the switch or fixture a few inches. If you have to run cable across framing members, make notches at each joist or stud (see page 33). Next, cut the holes for the switch and the fixture (see page 26).

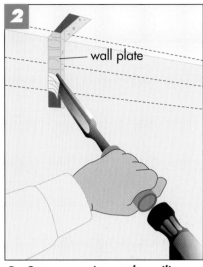

2. Cut an opening at the ceiling.
Where the wall and the ceiling meet, make a 1-inch-wide opening. Extend the opening at least 1 inch below the wall plate, and 2 inches at the ceiling. Chisel a channel into the framing deep enough to accommodate the cable.

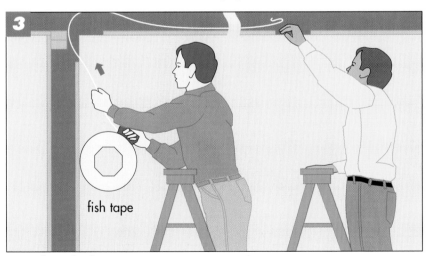

3. Fish to the fixture.
Slowly feed fish tape into the ceiling opening. If the tape meets resistance and coils up, pull back a few feet, shake the tape, and try again. Shaking also makes the tape rattle in the wall—a sure way to locate the tape. For longer runs, use two tapes, feeding in one from either end and snagging them together (see page 33).

4. Run cable to the switch.
Typically the wall cavity will be clear enough to push the cable down through the wall to the switch opening. Or, work a fish tape up, and pull the cable to the switch box opening. Staple the cable into the notches before patching the wall and ceiling.

RUNNING CABLE IN UNFINISHED SPACE

If you're working on a new addition, or if you've gutted a room and removed the old walls, running cable will be much easier. Begin by installing the electrical boxes. Place all the receptacles and switches at uniform height (12 to 18 inches from the floor for receptacles, 48 inches for switches). Make sure the boxes protrude forward from the face of the studs so your drywall will be flush with the front of them. Once the boxes are in place, bore holes in the middle of framing members.

YOU'LL NEED...

TIME: 1 hour to install two boxes and run 10 feet of cable.
SKILLS: Drilling holes, fastening boxes in place.
TOOLS: Drill with spade bit, hammer, chisel.

1. Bore the holes to run cable.
With an electric drill and a sharp ³/₄-inch spade bit, you can bore holes for a run of cable quickly. Have extra bits on hand for large jobs. Align the holes with each other by eye or use a chalk line to mark a guide. Bore as near the center of each stud as possible to maintain the strength of the framing and lessen the chance of drywall or trim nails piercing the cable. See Step 4 if the corners are solid wood.

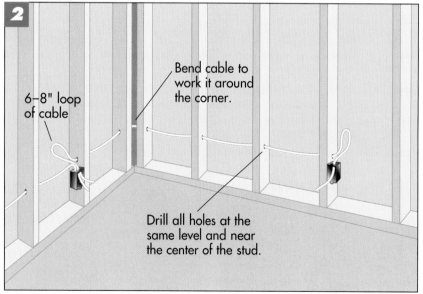

6–8" loop of cable

Bend cable to work it around the corner.

Drill all holes at the same level and near the center of the stud.

2. Run the cable.
Run the cable fairly tightly, so that it does not hang between studs. At the corners, you may need to bend the cable sharply to keep it at least 1¼ inches from the outer face of the framing. At each box, leave a loop of 6 to 8 inches of cable. This loop gives a margin of error if the wire is damaged when stripped, and makes future repairs and improvements easier.

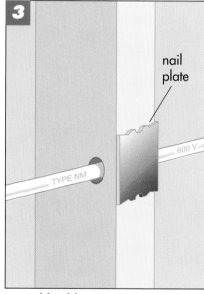

nail plate

3. Add cable protectors.
If some of the holes end up less than 1¼ inches from the face of a framing member, install a nail plate. Inexpensive and easy to install, it shields live electrical wires from being pierced by nails or screws. Simply tap the nail plate into place with a hammer.

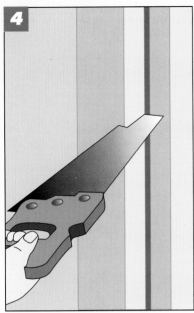

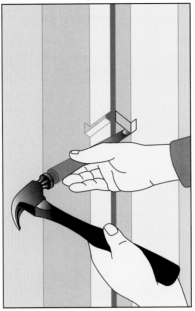

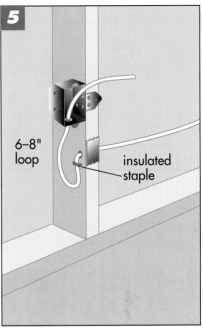

4. Cut notches at corners.
If the corner is solid wood you'll need to cut a notch to run cable around corners. Use a hand saw or a reciprocating saw to make two cuts in each stud, wide enough and deep enough for the cable to fit easily. Chisel out the wood between the two cuts. At inside corners, leave plenty of room—the cable cannot make sharp 90-degree turns. Cover each notch with a nail plate to protect the cable.

5. Tighten and attach the cable.
Pull the cable fairly taut as you install it. At each box, leave a 6- to 8-inch loop and attach the cable with an insulated staple.

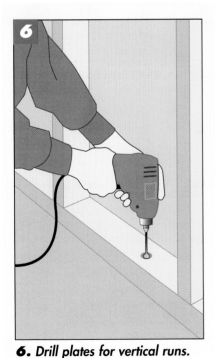

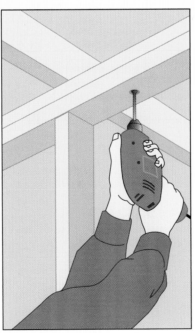

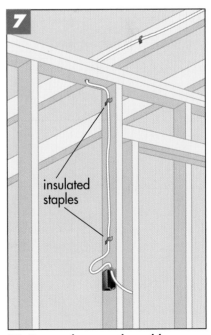

6. Drill plates for vertical runs.
Drill holes in top and bottom wall plates with a ¾-inch spade bit. Drill the holes near the center of the plates. If necessary, use a drill extension to bore through 2×4 plates. To avoid burning up the bit, stop periodically to let it cool. Drill at high speed and push gently.

7. Run and secure the cable.
On vertical runs, secure the cable with insulated staples every 4 feet or so, wherever you change direction, and 8 to 12 inches from each box. Avoid sharp bends in the cable.

RUNNING CABLE IN ATTICS AND FLOORS

How cable is run in an attic depends on how accessible and usable the attic is. Some local codes allow cable to be surface-mounted in seldom-used spaces. Cable can be attached to the top of the joists with insulated staples. Then 1×2 guard strips are nailed on either side. These strips will protect the cable from damage if anyone steps on it or sets a heavy object on it.

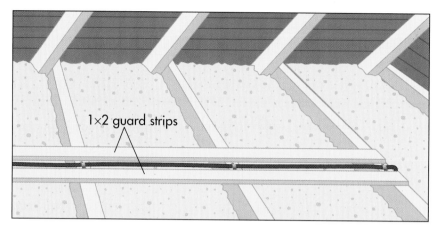

1×2 guard strips

Running cable through holes

If your attic is readily accessible, bore holes through the joists, at least 1½ inches below the top of the joists (see near right). For best protection—and to add a utilitarian floor—install plywood over joists. If the attic has flooring, remove some of it to install the cable, or take an alternate route along framing members. In a basement, cable should be run through holes in the joists.

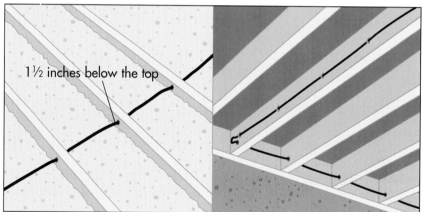

1½ inches below the top

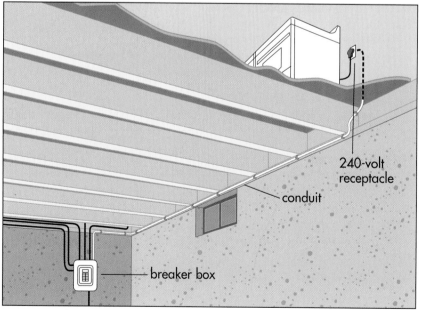

240-volt receptacle

conduit

breaker box

Strapping thicker cable

Because the heavy cable (8-gauge or larger) used for 240-volt appliance circuits is too stiff to thread easily through holes in joists, some towns allow wiring to be strapped to the underside of joists and along joist plates. Check your local code—conduit may be required for all exposed runs.

EXPERTS' INSIGHT

Special protection
Many special rules may apply when running cable in a permanently unfinished space. Check the local codes before you do any work. Some codes require that cable must be protected in an attic when it is within 6 feet of the entrance; in a garage or basement when it is within 8 feet of the floor. The most commonly accepted form of protection is conduit.

CONNECTING CABLE TO BOXES

*T*his page shows the most common systems for connecting nonmetallic cable to boxes. Other connectors are needed for metallic sheathed cable, Greenfield, and conduit (see pages 41 and 44). Leave ½ inch or more of sheathing inside the outlet box.

▶ Nonmetallic box with clamp

Some nonmetallic boxes come with internal clamps. However, clamping may not be necessary. Some local codes require only that the cable be secured within 8 inches of the box.

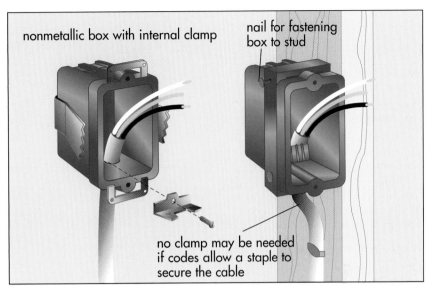

nonmetallic box with internal clamp

nail for fastening box to stud

no clamp may be needed if codes allow a staple to secure the cable

internal saddle clamp

holds 1 or 2 cables

◀ Metal box with saddle clamp

Some metal boxes come with internal saddle clamps. By tightening the saddle-clamp screw, one or two cables can be secured quickly.

▶ Metal box with clamp connectors

Remove a knockout hole in the box, insert a clamp connector into the hole, and secure it with a locknut. Slide the cable through the clamp connector and into the box. Tighten the saddle onto the cable. In some situations it is easier to clamp the connector to the cable first, then slide it into the box and screw on the locknut.

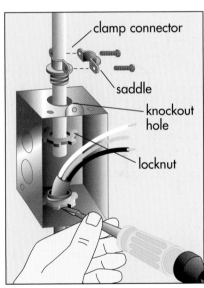

clamp connector

saddle

knockout hole

locknut

◀ Plastic connector

A plastic connector works like a clamp connector, but it is quicker and easier to use. Snap it into the knockout hole, insert 6 to 8 inches of cable, and tighten the capture screw. Other types grab the cable when you pry up on a wedge or squeeze the unit with pliers.

plastic connector

capture screw

connector snaps into knockout hole

▶ Quick clamp

Some boxes come with internal quick clamps. Pry up a spring-metal tab and slip the cable through. The clamp springs back by itself to hold the cable securely.

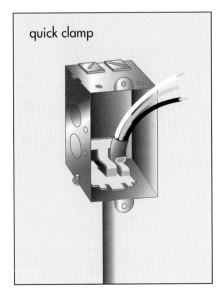

quick clamp

WORKING WITH BX, GREENFIELD

Flexible armored cable, or BX, is composed of a bendable metal sheathing containing insulated and ground wires. Greenfield, or flexible conduit, is a hollow flexible metal sheath. Like conduit, it is a tube through which wires are pulled. Check local codes regarding use of these materials—restrictions vary. (See page 19 for the different types of wire and cable available.)

CAUTION!
Whenever you work with these materials, you end up with cut ends that are sharp. If wires are allowed to rub against them, insulation could be stripped, resulting in an electrical short. Follow the procedures here carefully to protect wires at all times.

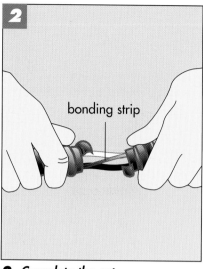

1. Cut notch in the sheathing.
To get through the metal covering, hold a hacksaw at a right angle to the spirals and cut partway through the armor. With BX, be especially careful not to nick the insulation on the wires inside. For a safe and easy way to cut cable, use a BX cutter (see inset above).

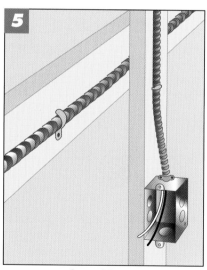

2. Complete the cut.
Twist the armor and it will snap free. The paper-wrapped wires (and aluminum bonding strip, if there is one) can be snipped with ordinary wire cutters. To expose the wires for connections to boxes and fixtures, cut off the armor at a second point about a foot away.

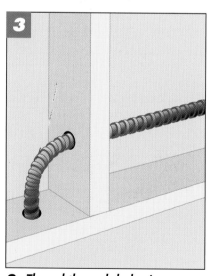

3. Thread through holes in framing members.
Run armored cable and flexible conduit through holes bored in the middle of framing members. Where necessary, use notches. BX and Greenfield are heavier and stiffer than nonmetallic cable, so it will take more room every time you want to change direction.

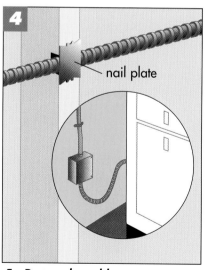

4. Protect the cable.
Even armored sheathing can be pierced with a nail, so anywhere that the cable is within 1¼ inches of the framing surface, protect it with a nail plate designed for the purpose. For short runs (see inset), flexible armored cable can be left exposed—check your local codes.

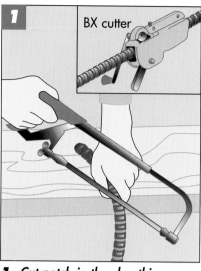

5. Secure the cable.
Support metal-clad cable with specially designed straps or staples every 4 feet or so and within 12 inches of boxes. If you're fishing through existing walls or ceilings, secure the run as best you can.

CONNECTING BX, GREENFIELD

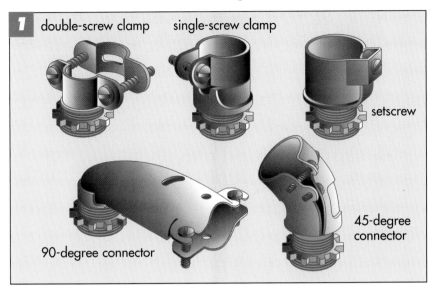

double-screw clamp   single-screw clamp

setscrew

90-degree connector

45-degree connector

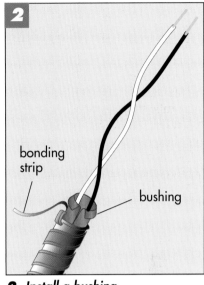

bonding strip

bushing

1. To connect cable to boxes, choose the connectors.

In most cases, use a simple straight connector that holds the cable in place either by clamping it or with a setscrew. In some tight situations, you may need to use a

90-degree or 45-degree connector. To install a connector, choose the side of the box you wish to access, and remove the knockout. Cut the cable to length and trim off the armored sheathing (see page 40).

2. Install a bushing.

Pull the brown paper surrounding the wires in BX back about an inch inside the armor. This leaves room to slip in a bushing. If your cable has a bonding strip, fold it back as shown.

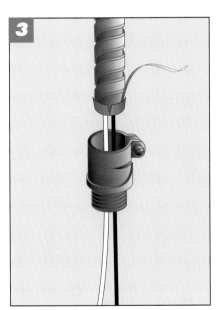

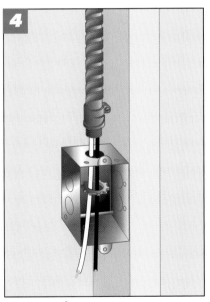

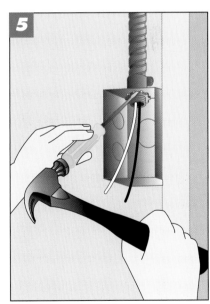

3. Attach the connector.

Slip on a connector, making sure the bushing is in place. Tighten the clamp or setscrew. Armored cable and conduit are self-grounding, so you don't need a grounding wire. Some codes require that the bonding strip be attached to the tightening screw.

4. Insert the connector.

Slip the wires and connector into a knockout hole, slip on a locknut, and tighten with your fingers. As with all wiring, connections should be made only in boxes.

5. Tighten the locknut.

Tighten the locknut with a hammer and screwdriver. Finally, tug on the cable to make sure everything is securely fastened.

CUTTING AND ASSEMBLING CONDUIT

Codes sometimes require conduit, especially for exposed areas. Conduit has definite advantages: It protects the wires well, and the electrical system can be upgraded later simply by pulling new wires through the conduit. Conduit is the most difficult way to install wiring because it's hard to bend. But it is still within the reach for do-it-yourselfers. For small jobs, use elbows and connectors at each turn to avoid bending conduit.

Codes allow many wires to be pulled through conduit. But the more wires you pull, the more crowded the conduit, so buy larger conduit than is required—say, ³/₄-inch instead of ¹/₂-inch.

YOU'LL NEED...

TIME: About 2 hours for a run with three bends and two boxes.
SKILLS: Careful measuring, clean cutting, screwing pieces together.
TOOLS: Tubing cutter or hacksaw, pliers, screwdriver.

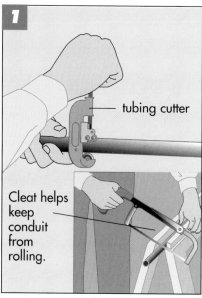

tubing cutter

Cleat helps keep conduit from rolling.

1. Measure and cut.
Measure the distance for the run—don't forget to subtract for the connector or elbow you will be using. Cut with a tubing cutter by clamping it to the conduit and rotating it a few times. Tighten and rotate until the cut is made. Or cut with a hacksaw. Hold conduit against a cleat, or use a miter box to keep it from rolling as you saw.

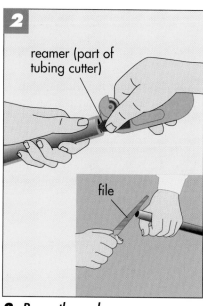

reamer (part of tubing cutter)

file

2. Ream the ends.
Sharp edges can chew up wiring insulation in a hurry. Remove all burrs and rough spots from the inside of the conduit, using the reamer that's attached to the tubing cutter or a file. File rough spots on the outside as well, so the conduit can slip easily into a connector.

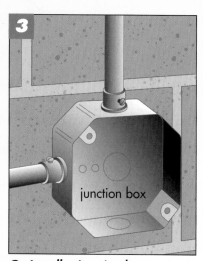

junction box

3. Install a junction box.
Where you have more than four turns to negotiate, install a junction box. When it's time to pull the wires, it will let you start another run. More boxes and few bends ease wire-pulling.

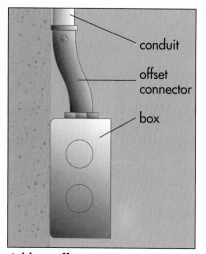

conduit

offset connector

box

Add an offset.
Use an offset connector to keep the conduit flush against the wall when it's attached to a box. The conduit can be bent to form an offset (see page 43), but adding an offset connector is easier.

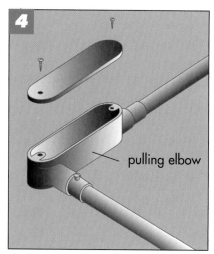

pulling elbow

4. Install pulling elbows.
A pulling elbow makes negotiating corners easier. Remove the cover to pull the wires through. Don't make any connections inside a pulling elbow; wires must pass through without a break.

BENDING CONDUIT

For larger jobs, it is expensive and time-consuming to use connectors at each corner. Instead, bend the conduit. Bending isn't difficult, but getting the bend in just the right location is tricky and requires some practice.

Runs begin and end at places where you can get at wires to pull them. Codes generally forbid a total of more than 360 degrees of bends in a run. Add up the degrees of the bends you'll be making in a single run before you start bending to ensure the total is less than 360 degrees.

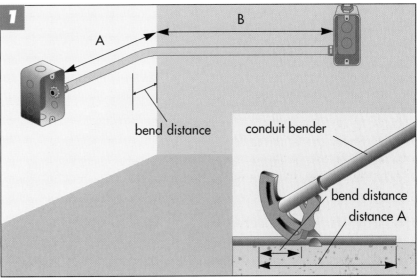

YOU'LL NEED...

TIME: About 30 minutes to measure, bend a piece, and connect it on either end.
SKILLS: This is a specialized skill that requires practice.
TOOLS: Conduit bender, tape measure, black marking pen.

1. Measure for a corner.
To get conduit around a corner, first measure from the box to the top of the bend (distance A). Then subtract the bend distance and mark the conduit. (The bend distance for $\frac{1}{2}$-inch conduit is 5 inches. For $\frac{3}{4}$- and 1-inch conduit, allow 6 and 8 inches, respectively.) Slip the conduit bender onto the tubing and align it as shown. After making the bend, trim section B by holding the bent conduit in place for measuring, and cutting the end so it just reaches the box.

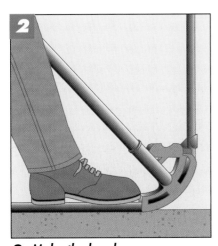

2. Make the bend.
With one foot on the rear of the bender, pull slowly and steadily on the handle. Be careful. Tugging too sharply will crimp the tubing and you'll have to start over again with another piece. (Codes forbid installing crimped conduit.) Making crimp-free bends takes practice, so don't be surprised if your first efforts fail.

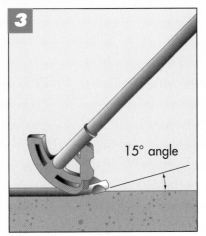

3. To form an offset, start with a 15-degree bend ...
When mounting conduit on a flat surface, you'll need to form an offset at each box. Offsets must be aligned with other bends in the tubing. A stripe painted along the length of the conduit helps you do this. First make a 15-degree bend.

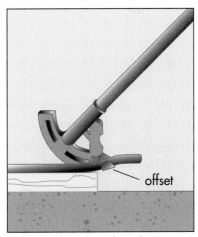

then bend in the other direction.
Roll the conduit over, move the bender a few inches farther from the end, and pull until the section beyond the first bend is parallel to the floor.

CONNECTING CONDUIT

1. Use couplings to join sections.
To join sections end to end, use either setscrew or compression couplings, securely fitted.

> **CAUTION!**
> Make all connections mechanically strong. Pulling wires through conduit can put a strain on connections. Grounding depends on secure metal-to-metal connections.

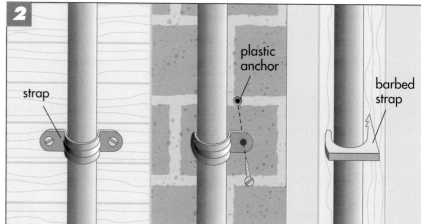

2. Anchor the conduit.
Anchor conduit runs with at least one strap every 8 feet and a strap within 3 feet of every box. For masonry walls, use screws and plastic anchors. When attaching to framing, simply drive barbed straps into the wood.

To mount conduit inside walls, bore holes in the studs (see page 32), or notch the framing and secure it with straps or metal plates every 8 feet.

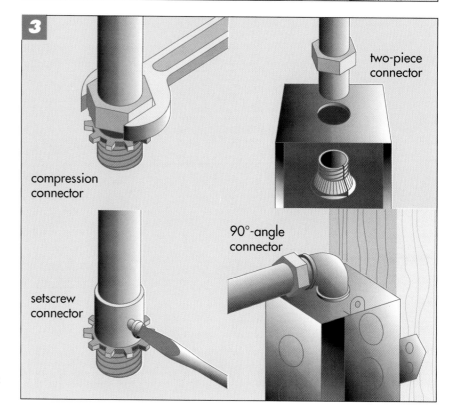

3. Connect to boxes.
The various types of box connectors differ mainly in the way they attach to conduit. Compression connectors grab the conduit as you tighten the nut with a wrench. To install a setscrew connector, slip it on and tighten the screw. Both types are available in 90-degree versions.

All these connectors attach to the box with the same threaded stud and locknut arrangement used with cable connectors (see page 39). Insert the stud into a knockout hole, turn the locknut finger tight, then tap the nut with a hammer and screwdriver to tighten it. A two-piece connector comes in handy when space is tight inside a box. Instead of a locknut, it has a compression fitting. As you tighten the nut, the fitting squeezes the conduit.

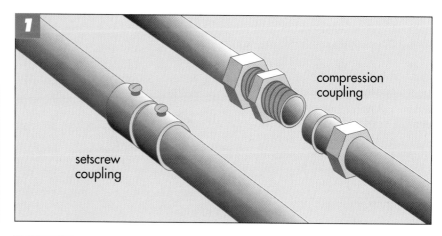

PULLING WIRE THROUGH CONDUIT

Now comes the moment when you realize why codes are so specific about bends, crimps, and burrs in conduit. Pulling wire can be surprisingly hard work. If you suspect that the wire is scraping against something that might damage the insulation, stop work, locate the trouble spot (you can find it easily by using the wire as a measuring device), and remove it. Purchase pulling grease, and lubricate the wires with it if you need to make a long pull.

YOU'LL NEED...
TIME: About an hour to pull cable through 60 feet of conduit.
SKILLS: Patience and some pulling muscle.
TOOLS: Fish tape, pulling grease, electrical tape.

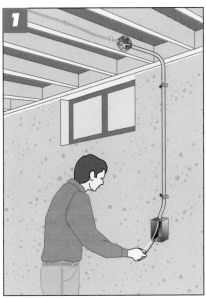

1. Push through short runs.
For short runs with only a couple of bends, you can probably just push the wires from one box to the other. Feed the wires carefully to protect the insulation.

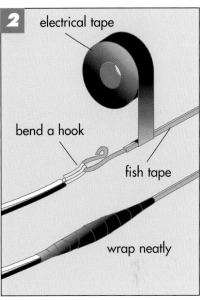

2. Attach a fish tape.
If you can't push the wires, you'll need a fish tape and an assistant. Snake the fish tape through the conduit, hook the wires to the fish tape and secure with electrician's tape. Wrap the connection neatly, so it can slide through the conduit.

3. Pull the wires through.
As one worker feeds the wire in and makes sure there are no kinks, the other pulls. Pull the wires with steady pressure—avoid tugging. As the wires work past bends, expect to employ more muscle. If you have lots of wires or a long pull, lubricate the wires with pulling grease. Where possible, use gravity to aid the process. Feed the wires from above and pull from below.

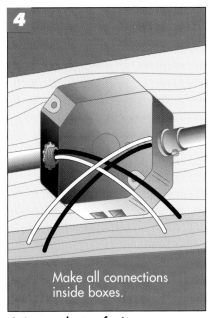

Make all connections inside boxes.

4. Leave plenty of wire.
Leave 6 to 8 inches of wire at each box. Never splice wire inside conduit—all wires must run continuously from box to box.

RUNNING WIRES UNDERGROUND

If you want to install a lamppost in the front yard or install new power to the garage, run the wiring underground.

Check local codes to see if you can simply run waterproof cable (labeled "UF") underground, or if you need to protect cable with conduit. Also find out how deep the wiring needs to be.

The potential for shock is greater outdoors, so buy watertight fittings designed for outdoor use. Protect all exterior receptacles with ground-fault circuit interrupters (see pages 76–77).

If you are installing only a light or two, you probably can extend power from an existing circuit. If the outdoor outlets will receive heavy use, you'll need to establish a new circuit. See pages 104–107 to assess the amount of demand you're likely to place on it.

YOU'LL NEED...

TIME: Two days to tap into an outlet, dig 30 feet of trench, and install a lamppost.
SKILLS: Making electrical connections, working with conduit, trenching, mixing and pouring concrete.
TOOLS: Wire stripper, lineman's pliers, conduit bender, and carpentry tools.

CAUTION!

Before you start digging trenches, contact your utility companies to find out where all the underground pipes and cables are in your yard.

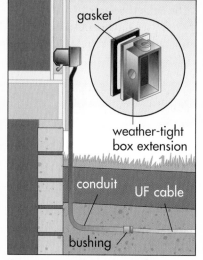

gasket

weather-tight box extension

conduit   UF cable

bushing

Tap an exterior receptacle ...
Add a weather-tight extension to an existing exterior receptacle, and run conduit from it. Attach it so the gasket will keep out moisture. Unprotected UF cable should exit from the conduit about 18 inches below grade through a special insulating bushing. Check to see if your local codes allow cable.

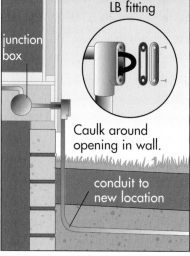

LB fitting

junction box

Caulk around opening in wall.

conduit to new location

or connect inside the house.
If no exterior receptacle is handy, find a nearby junction box, or run a new circuit from the service panel. At the point where the wiring leaves the house, install an LB fitting. Do not make connections inside the connector—wires must run from box to box.

Add a light to an existing switch.

If you want a lawn light that will come on when you turn on an exterior light, tap into an existing fixture. Remove the fixture from its electrical box and install a weather-tight box extension into which you can run the wiring. Run conduit down the side of your house, or hide cable inside the wall cavity.

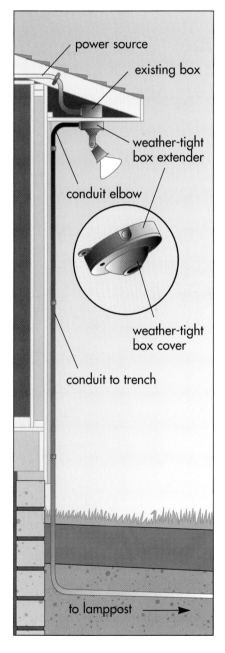

power source

existing box

weather-tight box extender

conduit elbow

weather-tight box cover

conduit to trench

to lamppost →

1. To install a lamppost, first dig a post hole and trench.

Various types of lampposts come with their own installation instructions. However, they all need to be firmly anchored to the ground. The simplest way to do this is to dig a deep post hole with a clamshell-type digger, set the post in it, and fill with concrete or tamped soil. If your trench must pass under a sidewalk or driveway, dig the trench on either side of the obstruction. Cut a piece of conduit about a foot longer than the span. Flatten one end to form a point. Drive the piece under and past the obstruction, cut off the flattened end, and connect it to conduit with couplings (see page 44).

2. Plumb the post.

After you run the wire (see page 45) and before you fill the hole, plumb and brace the post using scrap lumber. Attach the braces to the post with clamps, and screw or nail them to the stakes. Add water to premixed concrete, shovel it into the hole, and trowel smooth.

3. Make the electrical connection.

Wire the light (see page 68) using wire connectors (see page 30). A light-sensing photocell accessory switches on the light at nightfall. If you also wire it to a conventional indoor switch, the switch can override the photocell when the light isn't needed.

TIME-SAVER

DIGGING TRENCHES

For short runs where the digging is easy, a shovel will suffice, although you'll end up with a trench wider than needed. For large jobs, rent a walk-behind trencher, which makes a trench up to 2 feet deep. Give trees a wide berth to avoid damage to roots and time-consuming chipping.

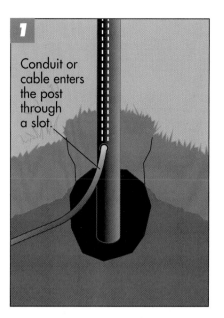

1 Conduit or cable enters the post through a slot.

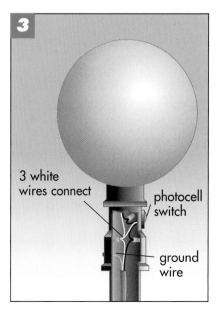

2 C-clamps

braces

stakes

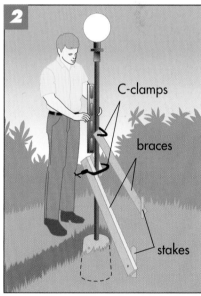

3 3 white wires connect

photocell switch

ground wire

REPLACING PLUGS AND CORDS

*F*aulty plugs pose the most common shock and fire hazards in the house. Plugs get stepped on, bumped against, and yanked out by their cords. It's a good idea to regularly inspect your plugs—especially if you have some old ones—for loose connections, damaged wire insulation, and prongs that have been bent so often they are in danger of breaking.

Fortunately, it is easy to replace faulty plugs to make your home significantly safer.

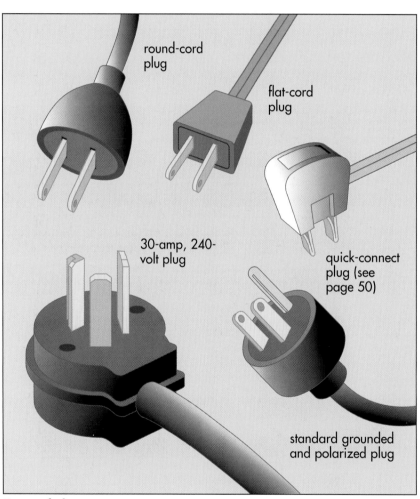

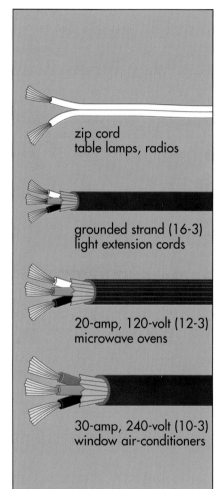

Types of plugs
Round-cord plugs often accommodate fairly thick wire and are used for moderately heavy appliances such as irons. Flat-cord plugs are suitable for lamps, radios, and other low-amperage devices. Newer lamp and extension cord plugs are polarized, with one blade wider than the other (see page 10).

Standard grounded plugs have a third, round prong for grounding; the two flat prongs are polarized.

Appliances that use 240 volts require heavy-duty three-pronged plugs of various configurations. The one shown here is for a 30-amp, 240-volt dryer.

Types of cords
For flexibility, cords have stranded, not solid, wire. Zip cord, so called because the two wires can be easily zipped apart, is for light duty. Use cords with 16-gauge wire for appliances pulling 15 amps or less and 12-gauge wire for 20 amps or less. For 240-volt appliances, use wire that is 10-gauge or thicker.

1. To replace a round-cord plug, strip and insert the cord.

Snip off the old plug. Remove the cardboard cover from the new plug, and slide the snipped-off end of the cord through. Strip off 3 inches of outer insulation and about ½ inch of wire insulation.

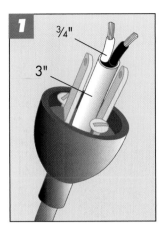

3/4"

3"

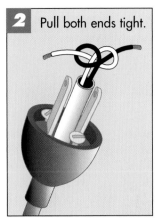

Pull both ends tight.

2. Tie Underwriters knot.

This special knot will ensure that tugging the cord won't loosen any electrical connections. Make the knot close to the end of the stripped outer insulation.

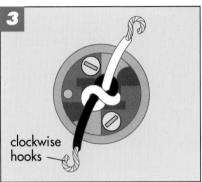

clockwise hooks

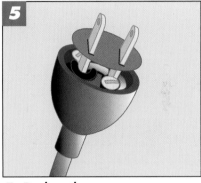

3. Bend hooks.

Twist the wire strands tight. With a pair of needle-nose pliers, shape clockwise hooks to wrap around the screw shafts.

4. Connect the wires.

Hook the wires on the screw shafts (attach the black wire to the brass-colored screw), and tighten. Tuck in stray strands.

5. Replace the cover.

Check to be sure all wires and strands are neatly inside the plug. Slip on the cardboard cover.

SAFETY

DON'T CHANGE THE PLUG TO FIT THE RECEPTACLE

■ If your appliance or tool has a plug with a third, round prong, then it should only be plugged into 3-hole outlets that are properly grounded (see page 10). If you remove the grounding prong, or if you use a plug adapter that is not connected to a ground, you will disable a feature designed to protect against electrical shock.

■ Some appliances and tools are "double insulated" and do not need the extra protection of a grounding prong. You can plug them into an ungrounded outlet and still be protected from shock.

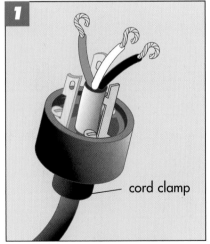

cord clamp

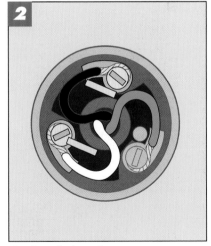

1. To repair a 240-volt plug, slide the plug onto the cord.

A 240-volt plug has a steel clamp that grips the cord, so you don't have to tie an Underwriters knot. Slide the plug onto the cord and strip about ½ inch of insulation from the ends of the three wires. Twist the strands tight, and use needle-nose pliers to form hooks.

2. Attach the wires.

Attach the black and red wires to brass-colored terminals, and the green one to the silver-colored terminal. Tuck in any loose strands as you tighten the terminal screws. Tuck all the wires in place, tighten the cord clamp, and slip on the cardboard cover.

WIRING QUICK-CONNECT, FLAT-CORD PLUGS

Keep a few quick-connect plugs on hand and you'll never again be tempted to put off replacing a faulty or questionable plug. Installing one is only slightly more difficult and time-consuming than changing a lightbulb.

Replacing a standard flat-cord plug is more like doing actual electrical work, but it takes only a little more time.

YOU'LL NEED...

TIME: About 5 minutes to install a quick-connect; 15 minutes for a flat-cord plug.
SKILLS: No skill at all for the quick-connect plug; stripping wire and connecting to a screw for the flat-cord plug.
TOOLS: Knife or scissors for the quick-connect; wire strippers and screwdriver for the flat-cord.

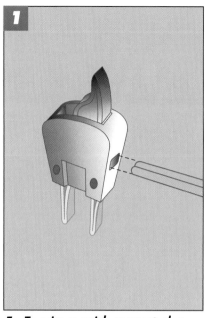

1. To wire a quick-connect plug, open the lever.
Snip off the old plug. Lift the lever on top of the new plug and insert the zip cord into the hole.

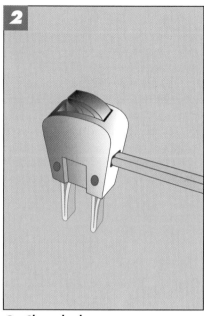

2. Close the lever.
Closing the lever pierces and holds the wire. Push the lever firmly down and you're done.

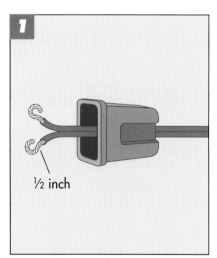

½ inch

1. To replace a flat-cord plug, slip on a shell and twist the wires.
Snip the old plug off, and slip the shell onto the cord. Peel apart the wires, and strip away about ½ inch of insulation. Twist the strands tight with your fingers, and use needle-nose pliers to form hooks that will wrap most of the way around each screw.

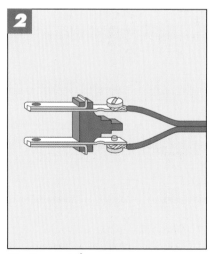

2. Connect the wires.
Wrap the wires clockwise around the screw threads, and tighten the screws to secure the connection. Tuck in any loose strands.

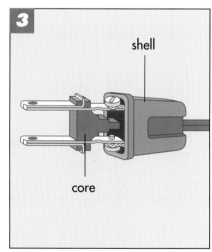

shell

core

3. Snap the shell on.
Grasp the shell of the plug and push the core toward it until it snaps into place. Put your appliance back into service.

REPLACING LAMP SOCKETS

Most standing lamps consist of a body, a base where the cord enters, a harp to support the shade, and a socket, which receives the cord at one end and the lightbulb at the other. The cord usually runs through a hollow threaded rod from the base to the socket.

When a lamp won't work and you know the bulb is OK, check the cord for damage. If the insulation is worn and cracked, replace the entire cord (see page 52). If the cord is OK, the problem is most likely in the socket.

Most lamps have felt bases that must be removed before repairing the lamps. Remove the felt by paring it off with a utility knife. After the repair, reapply the felt with white glue.

YOU'LL NEED...

TIME: About an hour to replace a lamp socket.
SKILLS: Stripping wire, connecting wire to screws.
TOOLS: Wire stripper, screwdriver, needle-nose pliers.

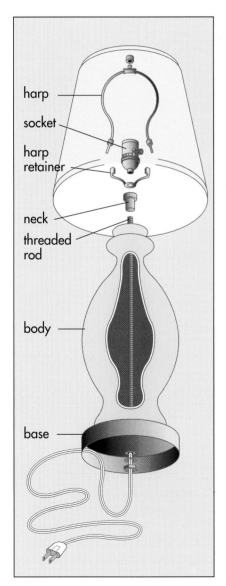

harp
socket
harp retainer
neck
threaded rod
body
base

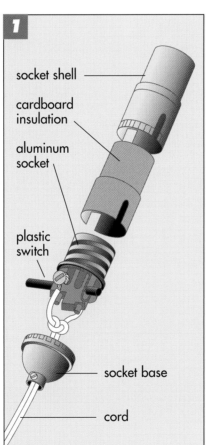

socket shell
cardboard insulation
aluminum socket
plastic switch
socket base
cord

1. Disassemble the socket.
Unplug the cord and remove the harp, if it is in the way. Examine the socket shell and find the word "press." Push hard here and the unit will pull apart into the components shown. Remove the cord from the socket.

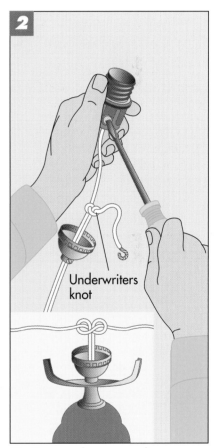

Underwriters knot

2. Connect the new socket.
Slip the new socket base onto the cord, and tie an Underwriters knot. Strip about ½ inch of insulation from the wires, twist the strands tight, and form them into hooks with a pair of needle-nose pliers. Wrap the wires clockwise around the shafts of the screws and tighten the screws. Reassemble the cardboard insulation and the outer shell. Attach the new socket to the lamp.

REWIRING LAMPS

Like plugs, lamp cords get stepped on and yanked. And if a lamp has a tendency to heat up, the cord's insulation can become cracked near the socket. Replace any cord with damaged insulation; it is dangerous.

Replacing a cord is not difficult. In fact, you may want to do it simply in order to have a cord that makes a lamp more attractive.

YOU'LL NEED...
TIME: About 45 minutes.
SKILLS: Stripping wire, connecting wire to screws.
TOOLS: Wire strippers, needle-nose pliers, screwdriver.

CAUTION!
UNPLUG IT FIRST!
Never work on a lamp or appliance while it is plugged in. Always unplug it first.

Pull cord through top.

Splice new cord to old to feed here.

1. Feed the new cord through.
Disconnect the old cord from the lamp socket, and snip off the plug. Tie the new cord to the old one with a piece of string or some tape. The trick is to make the connection thin enough so it slides through the center rod. Pull the new cord through as you withdraw the old one.

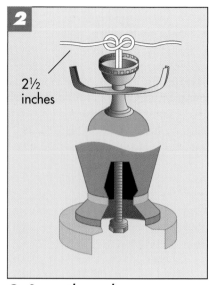

2½ inches

2. Secure the cord.
Snip off the old cord and discard it. Tie an Underwriters knot, as shown, leaving about 2½ inches of each wire to work with. Strip ½ inch of insulation from the end of each wire.

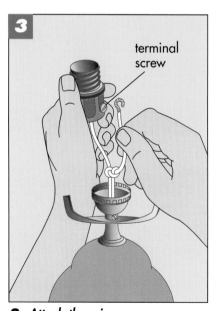

terminal screw

3. Attach the wires.
Twist the strands tight with your fingers. Use needle-nose pliers to form hooks, and wrap them around the terminal screws. Tuck any loose strands in as you tighten the terminal screws.

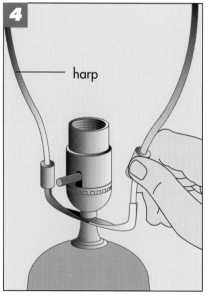

harp

4. Reassemble the lamp.
Reassemble the socket and install the harp as shown. Attach a new plug (see pages 48–50). You're ready to put in a bulb, attach the shade, and plug in your lamp.

CAUTION!
REPLACE DAMAGED LAMP CORD—DON'T TAPE IT
■ *It may not look dangerous, but nicked and cracked lamp wire insulation is the cause of many fires. Also, you or your children could receive painful shocks if you touch a bare spot.*
■ *If you see a damaged spot and need to keep using the lamp, wrap electrician's tape around the damaged area. But be aware that this is a temporary solution. The tape can easily come unwrapped. And if one part of the cord is damaged, chances are other parts are as well. Replace the cord as soon as possible.*

CHECKING INCANDESCENT FIXTURES

Though they vary widely in style, most incandescent fixtures have the same arrangement of components (see illustration, below right).

Mounting screws hold a canopy plate against the ceiling. The canopy has one or more sockets for bulbs. A translucent diffuser or globe cuts down on the glare of bare lightbulbs. In newer fixtures, a ring of fiber insulation provides added protection from heat damage to the wires and ceiling.

If a fixture shorts out, causing a circuit to blow and/or creating sparks, the problem is probably in the fixture. (If it simply refuses to light, the wall switch may be faulty. See page 56.)

YOU'LL NEED...
TIME: To inspect a typical fixture, about ½ hour.
SKILLS: No special skills needed.
TOOLS: Screwdriver.

CAUTION!
USE THE RIGHT BULBS
A label on the fixture will tell you the maximum bulb wattage allowed. Don't install higher-wattage bulbs or your fixture will overheat, burn up bulbs quickly, and become dangerous.

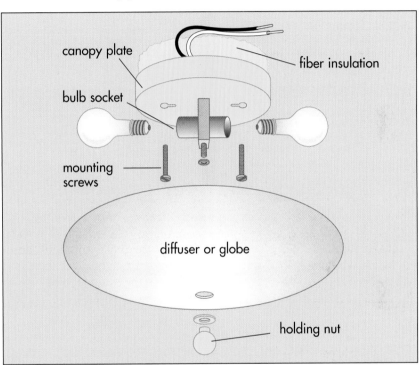

canopy plate

fiber insulation

bulb socket

mounting screws

diffuser or globe

holding nut

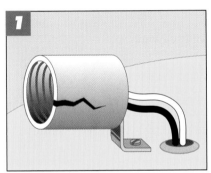

1. Inspect the socket.
Shut off the circuit that supplies power to the fixture. Inspect the socket. If it is cracked, or if its wires are scorched or melted, replace it or the entire fixture. If it's OK, remove the bulb and check the contact at the socket's base. If there's corrosion, scrape the contact with a flat screwdriver or steel wool, and pry up on it.

2. Check the wiring.
If the problem remains, shut off the circuit again, loosen or remove the mounting screws, and drop the fixture from its outlet box. Check for loose connections and for nicked insulation. If you see drywall paper that is slightly

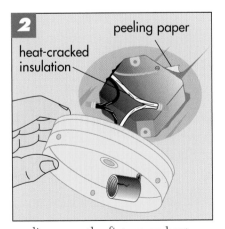

peeling paper

heat-cracked insulation

peeling near the fixture or heat-cracked wire insulation, your fixture is overheating, which means either that it is faulty or you need to reduce the wattage of the bulbs. Wrap any bare wires with electrical tape.

SAFETY

KEEP THE FIBER INSULATION
Although it makes installation a bit more difficult, don't remove the fiber insulation in the canopy plate. It provides extra protection against shorts.

TROUBLESHOOTING FLUORESCENT FIXTURES

The heart of a fluorescent fixture it its ballast, an electrical transformer that steps up voltage and sends it to a pair of lamp holders. The current passes through the lamp holders and excites a gas inside the fluorescent tube, causing its phosphorus-coated inner surface to glow with cool, diffused light.

Because they produce far less heat, fluorescent tubes last much longer than incandescent bulbs and consume considerably less electrical energy. However, problems with the fixtures sometimes arise. The ballasts burn out after years of steady use, and the lamp holders are easily cracked if they get bumped. Older units have starters that must be replaced periodically.

YOU'LL NEED...
TIME: To inspect a fixture and replace a ballast (for example), about an hour.
SKILLS: No special skills needed.
TOOLS: Screwdriver.

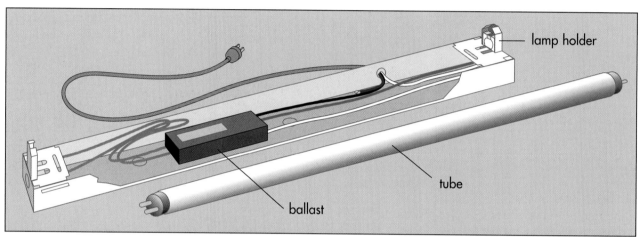

lamp holder

tube

ballast

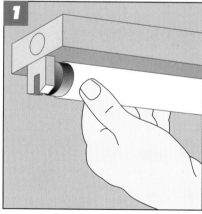

1. Wiggle the tube.
Rarely do fluorescent tubes burn out abruptly. If a tube suddenly stops lighting, try wiggling and rotating its ends to make sure it's properly seated.

CAUTION!
Never get rid of burned out tubes by breaking them. They contain mercury. Dispose of them whole, or request disposal guidelines.

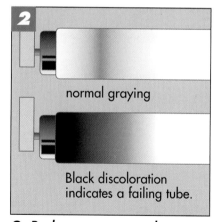

normal graying

Black discoloration indicates a failing tube.

2. Replace a worn-out tube.
A working tube usually has a grayish tinge near its ends. If the ends turn dark gray or black, it is failing and needs to be replaced. Purchase a tube that is the same length and wattage as the old one. If the tube is uniformly dim, it may simply need washing. To wash a tube, remove it from the fixture, wipe it with a damp cloth, and then replace the tube.

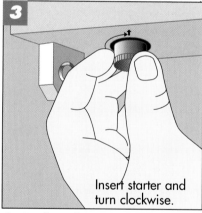

Insert starter and turn clockwise.

3. Replace the starter.
Older, delayed-start fluorescent lights flicker momentarily as they light up. If the flickering continues for more than a few seconds, make sure the starter is seated properly. Push it in and turn clockwise. When the ends of a tube light up but its center does not, the starter is defective. Press in and turn counterclockwise to remove it.

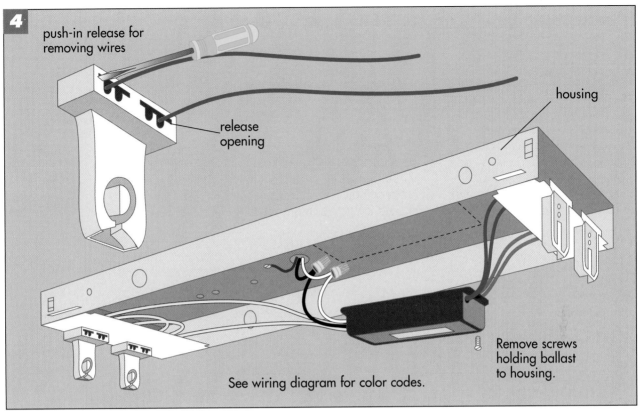

push-in release for removing wires

housing

release opening

See wiring diagram for color codes.

Remove screws holding ballast to housing.

4. Replace the ballast.

If the fixture hums or oozes a tarlike goop, the ballast needs replacing. (You may be better off replacing the entire unit. Compare prices.) **NOTE:** *Shut off the power.* To remove the ballast, release the wires at the sockets by pushing a screwdriver into the release openings. Unscrew the ballast and disconnect wires to power source. Reassemble with the new ballast.

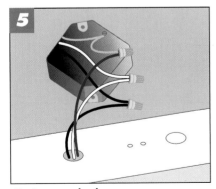

5. Inspect the box.

If none of these steps locates the problem, you may not have power going into the fixture. Remove the fixture, and look for loose connections and broken or bare wires in the outlet box.

EXPERTS' INSIGHT

TROUBLESHOOTING CHART FOR FLUORESCENT FIXTURES

Symptom	Solution
Tube does not light	1. Rotate the tube to make sure it is properly seated. 2. Replace any damaged lamp holders. 3. Replace starter, if there is one. 4. Check wall switch and outlet box to see that there is power to the fixture.
Tube flickers or only lights partially	1. Rotate the tube to make sure it is properly seated. 2. Replace any tubes that are discolored or have damaged pins. 3. Replace the starter, if there is one.
Black substance or humming sound	1. Replace the ballast or the entire fixture.

TESTING AND REPLACING SWITCHES

After getting flipped thousands of times, a switch can wear out. Unless the problem is a loose wire connection, there is usually no way to repair a faulty switch; you'll need to replace it.

It is easy to test switches and easy to replace them. If you want to replace your old switch with something more sophisticated—for example, a dimmer—check out the switch options presented on pages 16–17.

YOU'LL NEED...

TIME: About 30 minutes to test and replace a switch.
SKILLS: Using testers (we'll show you how); connecting wires to screw terminals.
TOOLS: Neon tester, continuity tester, screwdriver.

CAUTION!

Hold only the metal flanges of the switch when pulling it out of a box. Be very careful not to touch the terminal screws or to allow the screws to touch the edge of the box.

TOOL TIP

SAFE USE OF A CONTINUITY TESTER

Never use a continuity tester on wires that might be live. Always shut off power and disconnect wires before testing. The continuity tester uses a battery that generates a small current to test for the flow of electricity from one point to another. It is not made to carry household current.

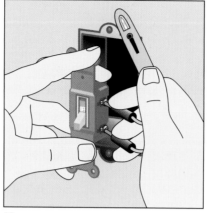

Use a neon tester ...
NOTE: *Shut off power.* Remove the cover plate and the screws holding the switch. Pull the switch out from the box. Turn the switch to OFF and restore power to the circuit. Touch the probes of a neon tester to the switch's screw terminals. If the tester glows, the box has power. Turn the switch on. Touch the probes to the terminals again. If the tester glows this time, the switch is blown and must be replaced.

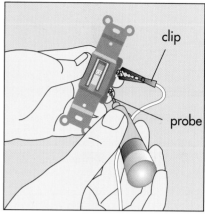

clip

probe

or use a continuity tester.
An easy way to test a switch is to use a continuity tester. Shut down the circuit leading to the switch, and remove the switch from the box—all wires should be disconnected. Attach the tester clip to one of the terminals, and touch the probe to the other. If the switch is working, the tester will glow when the switch is on and not glow when the switch is off.

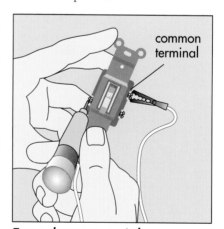

common terminal

Test a three-way switch.
To check out a three-way switch, shut off the circuit and attach the clip to the common terminal (it's usually labeled on the switch body). Touch the probe to one of the other screw terminals, and flip the switch. If it's OK, the tester will light when touching one of the two terminals. Flip the switch. The tester should light when the other terminal is touched.

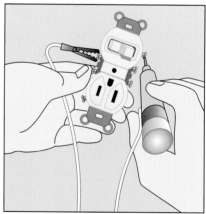

Test a switch/receptacle.
To test a device that has both a switch and a receptacle, attach the continuity tester clip to one of the top (switch) terminals and touch the probe to the top terminal on the other side. If the switch is working, the tester will glow when the switch is on, and not glow when it is off.

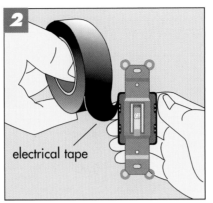

1. To replace a switch, remove the old switch.
If a switch is damaged, shut off power to the circuit, remove the screws holding the switch to the box, and gently pull out the device. Loosen the screw terminals and disconnect the wires.

2. Attach wires to the new switch.
Inspect the wires in the box, and wrap any damaged insulation with electrical tape. Attach the wires to the terminals of the new switch, and wrap electrical tape around the body of the switch, so the terminals are covered.

3. Reinstall the switch.
Carefully tuck the wires and switch back into the box, and connect the switch to the box by tightening the mounting screws. Don't force anything; switches crack easily.

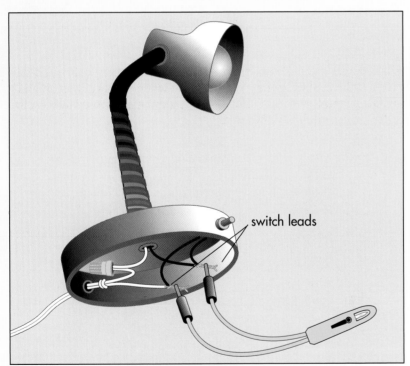

switch leads

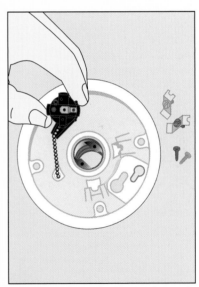

Test a fixture-mounted switch.
Small switches that mount on fixtures work by pull chain, flipping up and down, or twisting. These switches are not long-lived, so if the light does not work and the bulb is not blown, there is a good chance that the problem is with the switch. To test, shut off power to the fixture (or unplug it).

Remove the connectors holding the switch's leads. Leave the bare wires twisted together, and arrange them so the connections are not in danger of touching each other or anything else. Restore power to the fixture and carefully touch a neon tester to the connections. If the switch is turned on and the tester lights, the switch is bad.

Replace a fixture-mounted switch.
NOTE: *Shut off power.* Remove the fixture and disconnect the wires. Release the pull-chain switch by loosening the terminal screws and two screws in the base of the socket. Install a replacement switch and remount the fixture.

Other porcelain fixtures have an integrated switch. In such cases, replace the entire fixture. Lamp pull chains cannot be repaired. Buy a new pull-chain socket and replace the old one (see page 51).

TESTING AND REPLACING RECEPTACLES

Receptacles can be damaged in ways that are not readily apparent. Small cracks can lead to a short, and as they grow old, receptacles may hold plugs in place less firmly. The good news is that receptacles are inexpensive and easy to replace. Don't hesitate to replace one for any reason, such as because it is paint-glopped or the wrong color. However, if you want to replace your receptacle with one of a different type—for example, replace an ungrounded receptacle with a grounded one—read pages 10–11 and 18 first.

YOU'LL NEED...

TIME: About 5 minutes to test and 15 minutes to replace a receptacle.
SKILLS: Using a tester (we'll show you how), connecting wires to terminals.
TOOLS: Neon tester, receptacle analyzer, screwdriver.

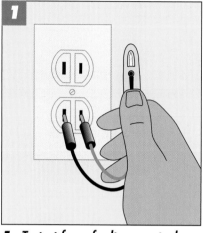

1. To test for a faulty receptacle, see if receptacle is live.
With the power to the circuit on, insert one probe of a neon tester into each slot of the receptacle. Do not touch the metal probes; only touch the insulated wires of the tester. If the tester glows, the receptacle is working. Test both plugs of a duplex receptacle.

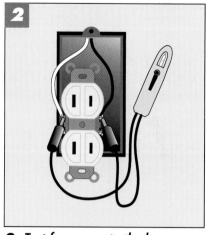

2. Test for power to the box.
If the receptacle is not live, check its power source. Shut off power to the outlet at the service panel, remove cover plate, disconnect the screws holding the receptacle to the box, and pull the receptacle out. Restore power, and touch one probe of the neon tester to a brass screw terminal and the other to a silver-colored terminal. The tester light will glow if power is coming to the receptacle.

1. To replace a receptacle, remove the old receptacle.
Shut off power to the box at the service panel. Note which wires are attached to which terminals. If necessary, make notations on pieces of tape and wrap them on the wires. Loosen the terminal screws and disconnect the wires.

2. Wire the new receptacle.
Inspect the wires in the box, and wrap electrical tape around any damaged insulation. Attach the wires to the receptacle, positioning each wire so it hooks clockwise on the terminal screw. Firmly tighten the terminal screws.

3. Wrap with tape and install.
Wrap the body of the receptacle with electrical tape, so that all the terminals are covered. Carefully tuck the wires and the receptacle into the box, and connect the receptacle to the box by tightening the mounting screws. Don't force the receptacle into place—it may crack.

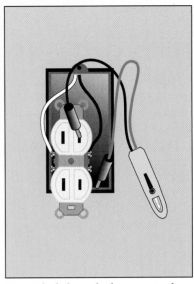

Test for grounding and polarization.

Do not turn off the power. Insert one prong of a neon tester into the short (hot) slot and the other into the grounding hole. If the tester glows, the receptacle is grounded and the slots are polarized. If the tester doesn't glow, put one probe in the grounding hole, the other in the long slot. If the tester glows, hot and neutral wires are reversed. If the tester doesn't glow in either place, the device isn't grounded.

Test a two-slot receptacle.

With the power on, insert one probe of a neon tester into the short (hot) slot, and touch the other probe to the cover plate screw (above left). The screw head must be clean and paint-free. Or, remove the cover plate and insert one probe in the short slot and touch the other to the metal box (above right). If the neon tester glows, the box is grounded, and you can install a

grounded three-hole receptacle.

If the tester doesn't glow, insert one prong into the long (neutral) slot and touch the other to the cover-plate screw or the box. If the tester glows, the box is grounded, but the receptacle is not correctly polarized; the hot and neutral wires are reversed. If the tester doesn't glow in either position, the box is not grounded. Do not install a three-hole receptacle.

TOOL TIP

USING A RECEPTACLE ANALYZER

With this handy device, you can perform a series of tests almost instantly without having to dismantle anything.

Leave the power on, but unplug all equipment and flip all switches to off on the circuit of the receptacle you will be testing. Plug the analyzer in. A combination of glowing lights will tell you what is happening with your receptacle (far right).

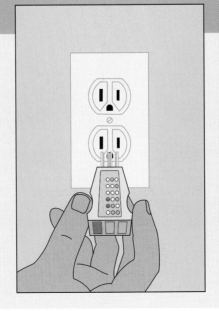

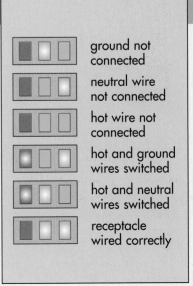

ground not connected

neutral wire not connected

hot wire not connected

hot and ground wires switched

hot and neutral wires switched

receptacle wired correctly

ADDING SURGE PROTECTION

Occasionally your electrical service can experience sudden increases in power, known as surges. A surge almost certainly will not harm lights and appliances, but it could damage sensitive electronic equipment, such as a computer.

To protect a few pieces of equipment, purchase a surge protector that simply plugs into an outlet. Or, you can replace an existing receptacle with a surge-protecting receptacle.

Install it as you would a normal receptacle, except that you will be connecting wires to wires rather than to screw terminals.

YOU'LL NEED...

TIME: About 15 minutes.
SKILLS: Joining wires.
TOOLS: Screwdriver, wire stripper, lineman's pliers.

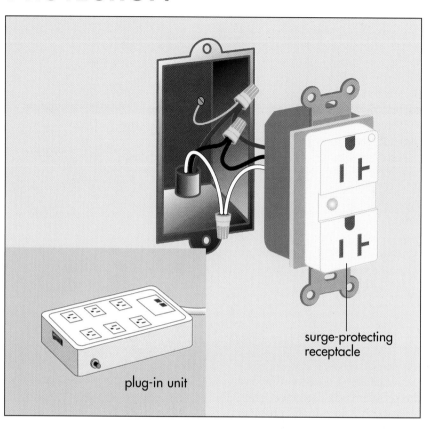

surge-protecting receptacle

plug-in unit

ADDING SURGE ARRESTERS TO CIRCUITS

To protect a circuit against surges, install this device in your service panel. At the service panel, shut off the main circuit breaker, and take off the panel cover. Remove the ½-inch knockout that is nearest to the circuit you want to protect. Insert the surge arrester through the knockout hole, and fix it in place by tightening the nut. Wire as shown, connecting the white wire to the neutral bus bar and the black wire(s) to breakers. Before connecting, cut wires as short as possible for maximum protection.

YOU'LL NEED...

TIME: About an hour.
SKILLS: Understanding of your service panel.
TOOLS: Screwdriver, tongue-and-groove pliers, wire stripper.

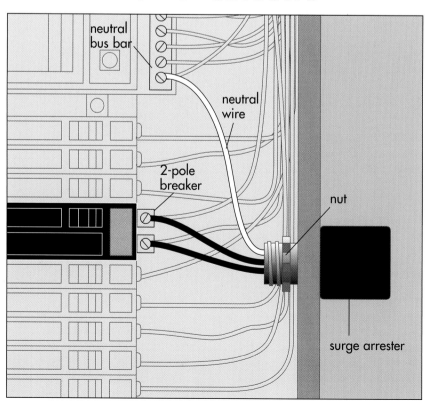

neutral bus bar

neutral wire

2-pole breaker

nut

surge arrester

TROUBLESHOOTING CIRCUIT BREAKERS

Think of a circuit breaker as a heat-sensing switch. As the illustrations at right show, when the toggle is on, current flows through a set of contacts attached to a spring and lever. The contacts are held together by tension in the bimetal strip through which the current flows.

If there is a short or an overload in the circuit, the bimetal strip heats up and bends. As it bends, it releases a lever that opens the spring-loaded contact. The contact remains open until the toggle is manually reset by the homeowner.

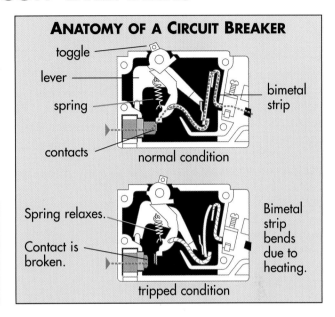

ANATOMY OF A CIRCUIT BREAKER

toggle
lever
spring
contacts
bimetal strip
normal condition

Spring relaxes.
Contact is broken.
Bimetal strip bends due to heating.
tripped condition

YOU'LL NEED...
TIME: A few seconds to reset a breaker; about 10 minutes per device to inspect for shorts.
SKILLS: No special skills needed.
TOOLS: Screwdriver.

Identify a tripped breaker.
A tripped breaker will identify itself in any of the four ways shown at left. To find out whether the problem has corrected itself, reset the breaker. If the problem persists, the breaker will shut itself off again. Usually the problem is an overload, and you only need to unplug or turn off one of the circuit's big energy users. If the circuit breaker keeps tripping even though it isn't overloaded, suspect a short. A defective plug, cord, or socket may be the problem.

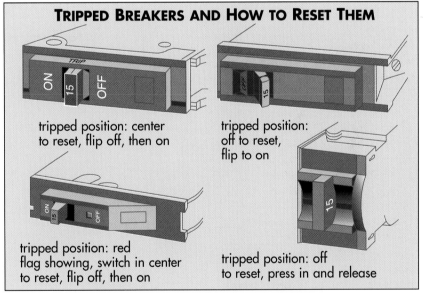

TRIPPED BREAKERS AND HOW TO RESET THEM

tripped position: center to reset, flip off, then on

tripped position: off to reset, flip to on

tripped position: red flag showing, switch in center to reset, flip off, then on

tripped position: off to reset, press in and release

Check connections in boxes.
Short circuits can occur in electrical boxes. Here, a wire has pulled loose from the switch and has shorted out against the box.

wire pulled loose

frayed insulation

Inspect wiring.
Frayed or nicked insulation will expose wire and could cause a short. Wrap damaged insulation with layers of electrical tape.

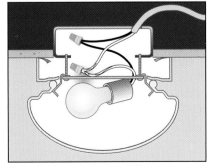

Watch for overheated fixtures.
High-wattage bulbs can melt insulation. Never use bulbs with higher wattage ratings than those for which the fixture is rated.

TROUBLESHOOTING FUSES

Fuses serve the same purpose as circuit breakers, but instead of tripping as a breaker does, a fuse contains a strip of metal that melts when too much current in the circuit produces heat. When this happens, you must eliminate the short or overload (see page 61), and replace the blown fuse.

YOU'LL NEED...
TIME: 10 minutes to inspect your fuses.
SKILLS: Using continuity tester.
TOOLS: Continuity tester, fuse puller.

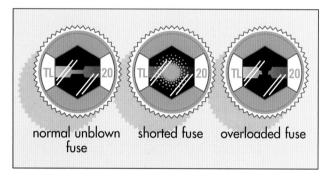

normal unblown fuse · shorted fuse · overloaded fuse

Understanding blown fuses
By examining a fuse you usually can tell what made it blow—an overload or a short. A short circuit usually explodes the strip, blackening the fuse window. An overload usually melts it, leaving the window clear.

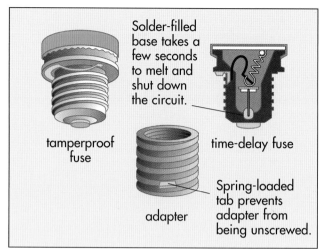

Solder-filled base takes a few seconds to melt and shut down the circuit.

tamperproof fuse · time-delay fuse · adapter · Spring-loaded tab prevents adapter from being unscrewed.

Fuse options
A tamperproof fuse is an important safety device that makes it impossible to install a fuse with a higher amperage rating than the circuit is designed for. It comes with a threaded adapter that fits permanently into the box. The adapter accepts only a fuse of the proper rating.

When an electric motor on a washing machine or refrigerator starts up, it causes a momentary overload, which can blow fuses unnecessarily. A time-delay fuse avoids this problem by not blowing during the surge. Only a sustained overload will blow the fuse.

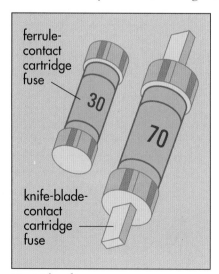

Cartridge fuses
Fuses for 30- to 60-amp circuits typically are the ferrule-contact cartridge type. Knife-blade-contact fuses carry 70 amps or more. Handle both with extreme caution. Touching either with your bare hand could fatally shock you.

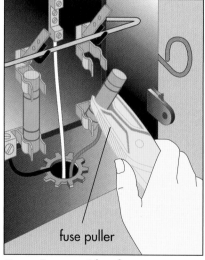

Removing cartridge fuses
For safety, keep a plastic fuse puller with your spare fuses, and use it as shown. Note, too, that the ends of a cartridge fuse get hot, so don't touch them immediately after you've pulled the fuse.

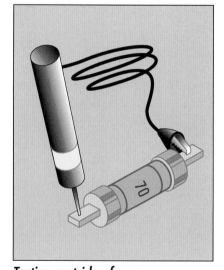

Testing cartridge fuses
To see if a cartridge fuse has blown, check it with a continuity tester. Clamp or hold the clip on one end, and touch the probe to the other. The bulb will light if it is not blown.

REPAIRING OR REPLACING DOORBELLS

A doorbell system starts with a transformer, which reduces current from 120 volts to somewhere between 6 and 30 volts. From the transformer, light-gauge wire connects the bell, chime, or buzzer with the back in a circuit that is usually open at the button. Pressing the button, which is a spring-loaded switch, closes the circuit and sends low-voltage power to activate the bell, chime, or buzzer.

If your bell does not work, find the cause by using the process of elimination described in the steps below. A voltmeter or multitester will make the job easier, but you also can do most tests with a short piece of bell wire or a screwdriver.

Unless you are working on the transformer, there's no need to shut off power while inspecting a bell. The voltage coming from the transformer is so low you will barely feel it.

YOU'LL NEED...

TIME: You may find and solve the problem in minutes, or it could take several hours.
SKILLS: Using continuity tester, ability to work methodically.
TOOLS: Voltmeter or multitester, screwdriver, short length of wire.

1. Check wires to the button.

To check a doorbell system, remove the button, turn it over, and examine the connections. To make sure that the wires cannot accidentally slip back through the hole, attach a spring clip. Scrape away any corrosion on the terminals. Tighten the connections to the terminals. Wrap any faulty insulation with electrical tape.

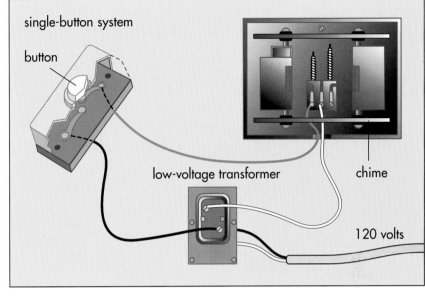

single-button system

button

low-voltage transformer

chime

120 volts

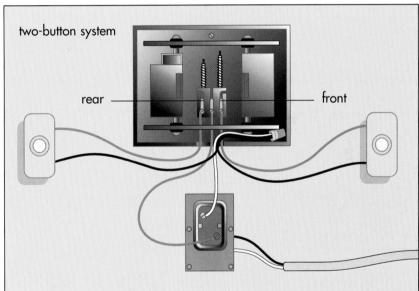

two-button system

rear

front

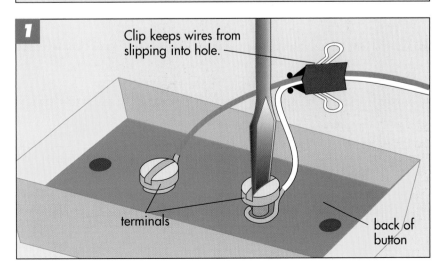

1

Clip keeps wires from slipping into hole.

terminals

back of button

Repairing or Replacing Doorbells *(continued)*

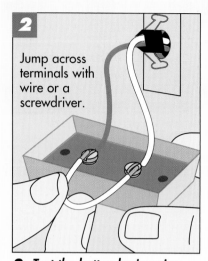

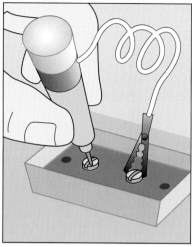

2. Test the button by jumping …
Weather and abuse make buttons the most vulnerable parts of a bell system. Test a button by jumping its terminals with a short piece of wire, as shown above. If the bell sounds, the button is faulty and should be replaced.

or use a continuity tester.
You can also test the button by disconnecting the wires and touching both terminals with a continuity tester. If the tester glows when the button is pressed, the button is working. If the bell still doesn't sound, disconnect the button, twist its wires together, and test further.

3. Check wires to the transformer.
Find your transformer. It may be near your home's service panel or attached to a junction box in the vicinity of the door or the bell. Look for corrosion, wires that have come loose, or faulty insulation.

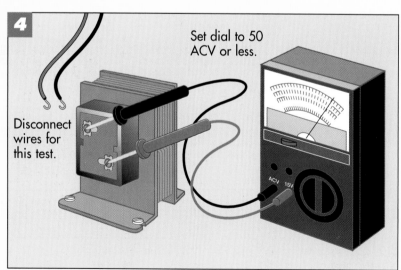

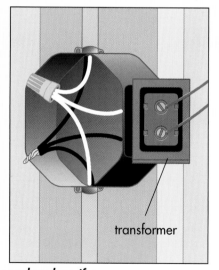

4. Test the transformer …
To check the transformer, disconnect both wires and touch each terminal with the probes of a voltmeter or multitester. Set the dial at ACV 50. If the meter shows no current at all, the

transformer is the culprit and should be replaced. You also can test a transformer by jumping the low-voltage terminals with a screwdriver. If you see a weak spark, it is OK.

and replace if necessary.
NOTE: *Shut off the power.* Remove the cover plate of the electrical box, remove the transformer, and disconnect the wires. Wire the new transformer just like the old one, and reassemble the bell.

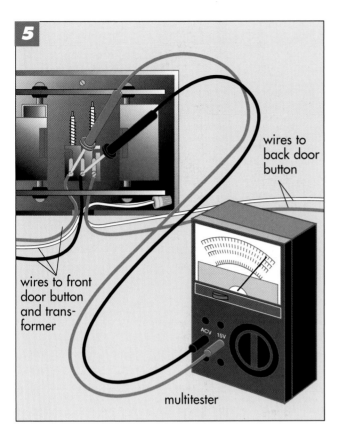

wires to back door button

wires to front door button and trans-former

multitester

5. Inspect the bell.

If the button, the wires, and the transformer are not to blame, check the bell itself. Remove the cover. Look for loose or broken connections. Even if you don't have a second button, the chime will have terminals labeled front and rear. Touch the voltmeter or multitester probes to the front and trans (meaning "transformer") terminals. If the meter registers a reading, then power is going to the bell, but the bell is defective. If you have a rear button, test again, touching rear and trans.

If you don't have a voltmeter, test the bell by removing it and temporarily wiring it directly to the transformer. If it is working, it will ring.

EXPERTS' INSIGHT

IF EVERYTHING IS OK, IT'S THE WIRES

If the button, transformer, and chimes check out, a wire likely has broken. Disconnect wires going into the bell, and test current flow with a voltmeter or multitester. Or, touch the front and rear wires to the transformer wire, and look for a spark. To run low-voltage wiring, see pages 106–107.

REPLACING CHIME UNITS

When shopping for a doorbell, consider your wall: Will the new unit cover up the discolored area left by the old one, or will it require you to do some touch-up painting? Make sure the doorbell you choose has the same voltage rating as its transformer.

TIME-SAVER

INSTALL A REMOTE-CONTROLLED CHIME

Running new wires is a time-consuming job. If you have damaged wires, consider installing a remote-controlled bell. This type costs more than a regular unit, but saves you the trouble of running wires.

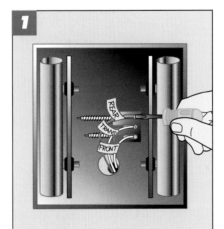

1. Label wires and remove chime.

Shut off power to the circuit if you like, but it's not necessary because the voltage is so low. The terminals are labeled, so label the wires the same as you disconnect them. These labels also will prevent the wires from accidentally slipping through the hole and into the wall. Unscrew the chime from the wall, and remove it.

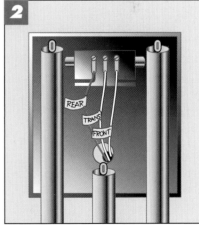

2. Install the new chime.

Attach the new chime to the wall with mounting screws. Use plastic anchors if you cannot drive a screw into a stud. Connect the low-voltage wires to the terminals, and attach the cover.

TROUBLESHOOTING THERMOSTATS

A thermostat is a switch that senses temperature and turns your heater or air-conditioner on and off accordingly. Most homes have low-voltage units like the one described here. A transformer reduces power from 120 volts to around 24 volts and sends it to the thermostat. Some systems have two transformers, one for heating and one for air-conditioning.

Possible causes of thermostat problems include faulty wiring, a corroded thermostat, and a worn-out transformer.

YOU'LL NEED...

TIME: Most inspections and repairs can be done in an hour.
SKILLS: No special skills needed.
TOOLS: Voltmeter or multitester, continuity tester, screwdriver, artist's brush, short piece of wire.

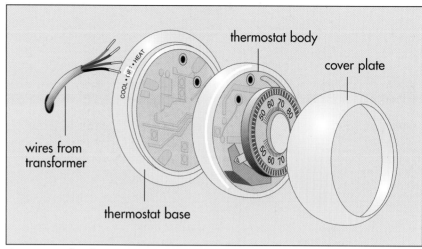

wires from transformer

thermostat body

cover plate

thermostat base

Anatomy of a thermostat
A low-voltage system begins with a transformer that is either mounted to a panel on the furnace or connected to an electrical box. Anywhere from two to six thin wires (depending on how many items are being controlled) lead to the thermostat base, where they are connected to terminals. The thermostat body contains the heat-sensing device and the control dial. Because the voltage is so low, it is not necessary to shut off power to the thermostat while working on it—unless you are working on the transformer.

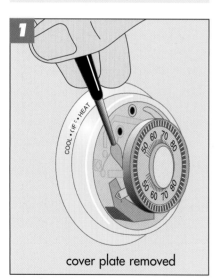

cover plate removed

1. Clean the thermostat.
Dust can cause a thermostat to malfunction. Remove the cover plate and brush the inner workings with an artist's brush. Pay special attention to dust and dirt on contacts.

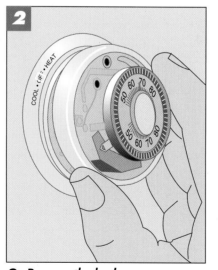

2. Remove the body.
Unscrew the screws that hold the thermostat body to the base, and pull the body away. Check to see that the base is securely fastened to the wall. If it is loose, the thermostat could tilt, which would throw off the settings. Blow on the body to remove more dust, but do not handle the parts inside—they are sensitive.

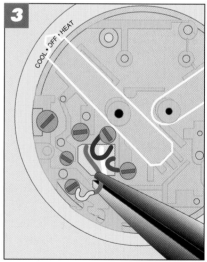

3. Inspect connections to the base.
Look for loose, corroded, or broken wires coming into the base. If any are damaged, clip them, strip insulation from the ends, and reattach. Tighten all the terminal screws to make sure the connections are secure.

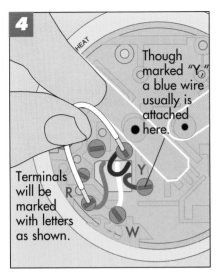

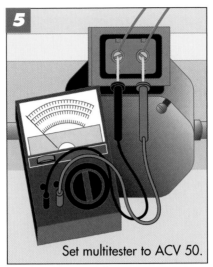

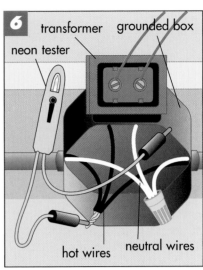

Set multitester to ACV 50.

4. Hot-wire the terminals.
Cut a short piece of wire, and strip insulation from both ends. Use it to "jump" between terminals. Touch one end to the "R" terminal and one to "W," and the heater's burner should come on. Touch "Y" and "G," and the fan should come on. If they do, the thermostat is faulty and should be replaced.

5. Test the transformer.
If the thermostat checks out, test the transformer. Touch one probe of a voltmeter or multitester to each of the low-voltage terminals on the transformer. Set dial to ACV 50. If the meter does not detect current, the transformer is defective and needs to be replaced.

6. Check power to transformer.
Before you go out and buy a new transformer, open up the transformer box and make sure that there is power leading to the transformer. Touch one probe of a tester to the hot wires and the other to the box (if grounded) or the neutral wires.

Installing a Programmable Thermostat
A programmable thermostat automatically changes the temperature in your home for sleeping and waking hours. It also can deliver different temperatures when you're away.

There are many options to choose from. Some control heat only, and some also control air-conditioning. Some can be completely programmed in one sitting; others require a week-long run-through.

When shopping for a new thermostat, bring along the brand name and model number of your old thermostat and the heating and air-conditioning units to make sure they'll be compatible. Here are guidelines for installation, but follow the manufacturer's instructions that come with the unit.

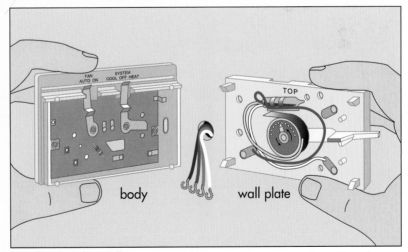

Removal and installation
As you remove wires from the old thermostat, label them. Remove the old thermostat. Pull the wires through the new wall plate, and mount the plate securely to the wall. Check that it is level. Push any excess wire back into the wall and hook up the wires according to the manufacturer's instructions.

Attach the body to the cover plate. Set the clock and program the unit according to the manufacturer's instructions. Attach the cover.

HANGING CEILING FIXTURES

Dramatically change the appearance of a room by adding or replacing a ceiling light. Although the choices are many, from simple ceiling fixtures to elaborate chandeliers, all are installed in essentially the same way: Power is drawn from a ceiling-mounted box designed to support a particular fixture. If you are replacing a ceiling fixture, take the time to inspect the wires and the area around the outlet box for heat damage (see page 53).

YOU'LL NEED...

TIME: An hour to mount a simple fixture; more time is needed for elaborate units.
SKILLS: Basic carpentry and wiring skills
TOOLS: Screwdriver, pliers.

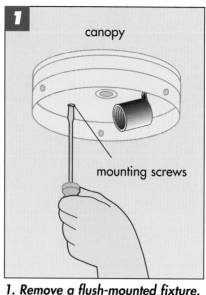

1. Remove a flush-mounted fixture.
NOTE: *Shut off the power.* Remove the globe or diffuser, and the bulb(s). Remove the screws or the cap nut holding the canopy in place, and drop the fixture down. Disconnect the black and white wires. Check wires for cracks in the insulation. To replace wire, see pages 32 through 38.

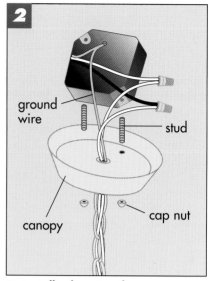

2. Install a hanging fixture.
This hanging fixture attaches with a pair of studs screwed to the box. Connect the black and white wires and the ground wire, coil them up into the box, and push the canopy into place so the studs poke through. If the unit does not easily push up flush to the ceiling, drop it down and rearrange the wires. Secure the canopy by twisting cap nuts onto the studs.

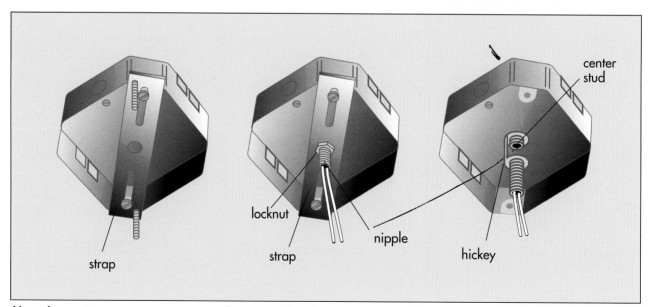

Mounting systems
If the holes in the canopy don't match those in the box, choose from the three mounting systems shown above. Adapt the box for fixtures with side mounting bolts by fastening a **strap** to the box. Some straps have several screw-in holes to choose from. For center-mounted fixtures, screw a **nipple** into the center hole of a strap, and secure it in place with a locknut. If the box has a center stud, attaching a **hickey** is another way to adapt the box.

INSTALLING TRACK LIGHTING

*T*rack lighting gives you a great deal of flexibility. After it is installed, you easily can change the number of lights, their positions or the direction they point—even the type of light.

The initial hookup is much like other ceiling fixtures (see page 68). But installing the tracks themselves involves measuring your ceiling and establishing lines for correct placement, so the track is pleasingly aligned with your room. Have two ladders and one helper on hand for placement. (If you do not have an existing box to tie into, see pages 32–39.)

YOU'LL NEED...

TIME: If you are working from an existing ceiling box, 4–6 hours for a 12-foot system.
SKILLS: Connecting wires in a box, careful measuring of and attaching to a ceiling.
TOOLS: Tape measure, Phillips screwdriver, drill with screwdriver bit.

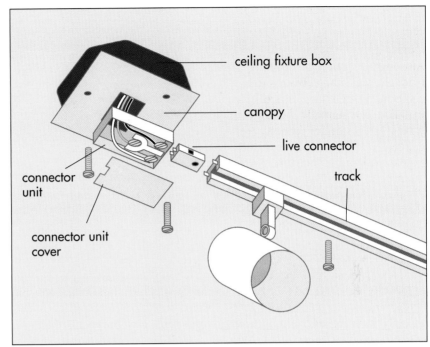

How track lighting goes together.
Instructions for your unit will tell you specifically how to make connections, but most track lights go together in the following way. A connector unit connects to the ceiling electrical box and transfers power to the tracks. Inside the tracks are two metal strips that run along its length. They are electrified by wires from the box. The lights themselves have two contacts at their base. When the contacts meet the electrified strips, the light comes on. A connector cover caps off the connector unit.

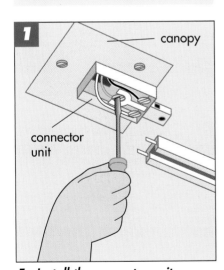

1. Install the connector unit.
NOTE: *Shut off the power.* Attach the black, white, and ground wires from ceiling fixture box to the connector unit terminals. Hook wires clockwise on the screw shafts before tightening. Fasten the connector unit to the canopy.

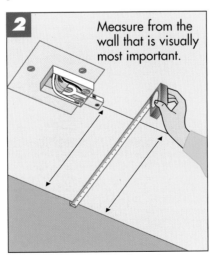

2. Lay out and install tracks.
To establish a line that the track will follow, measure off a wall at several points, and strike a line between them. Connect the track to the connector plate. Screw the track into ceiling joists, or use toggle bolts.

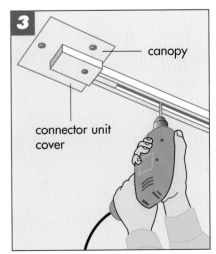

3. Install lights and attach cover.
Restore power to the circuit. Install lights according to instructions—in most cases, you twist them in place. Attach the canopy and any connector covers by snapping into place.

INSTALLING RECESSED CEILING LIGHTS

Recessed fixtures have much to recommend them: They are inexpensive, unobtrusive, and if you have no fixture box already in place, a recessed light is the easiest fixture to install because it comes with a box attached. Purchase a unit with a silver reflector for greater brightness, or choose a black reflector for more subdued lighting. Make sure the fixture you buy will fit in your ceiling space. If your ceiling joists are smaller than 2×10, for instance, you will need a fixture with a side-mounted box.

YOU'LL NEED...

TIME: After running cable from the switch, about 1½ hours.
SKILLS: Cutting a clean hole in the ceiling, attaching wires.
TOOLS: Keyhole saw, screwdriver, drill with screwdriver bit.

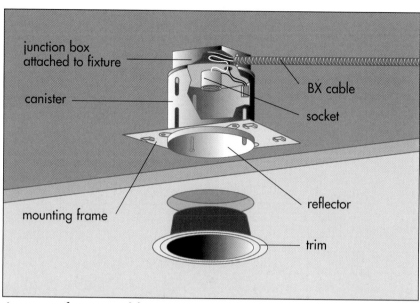

Anatomy of a recessed fixture
Designed for installation where there is no access from above (a common problem when adding recessed lighting in the first-floor ceiling of a two-story house), this unit sits atop drywall or plaster. The fixture can be installed from below. The mounting frame spreads out the weight of the unit.

CAUTION!
KEEP IT COOL

If you don't take precautions, a recessed light can build up a lot of heat, which can lead to prematurely burned-out bulbs, damage to your ceiling, melted wire insulation, and even danger of fire. Allow the fixture room to breathe. Keep any ceiling insulation at least 3 inches away from it, and don't place it in a cramped space. Use bulbs of the recommended type and wattage. You can increase the wattage if you use a floodlight bulb because it directs more heat away from the fixture than a regular bulb. Don't leave any flammable materials, such as scraps of insulation paper, anywhere near the fixture.

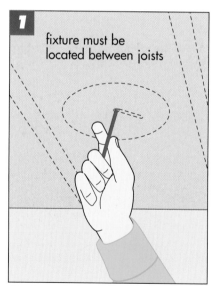

1. Cut a hole.
Determine the general location of the fixture, and drill an exploratory hole. To make sure a joist is not in the way, use a bent wire, so when spun it will follow the circumference of the fixture. If the site is clear, mark and cut an opening with a keyhole saw.

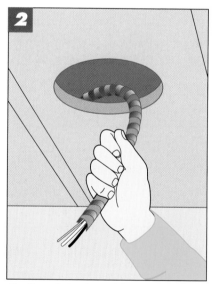

2. Rough in the wiring.
NOTE: *Shut off the power.* For the rough wiring, simply run cable to the hole where the fixture will go. Leave a foot or so of extra cable sticking through the hole. See pages 84–90 for ways to wire a switched ceiling fixture.

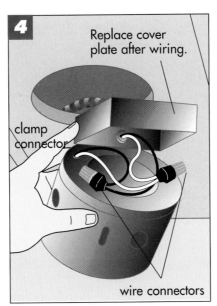

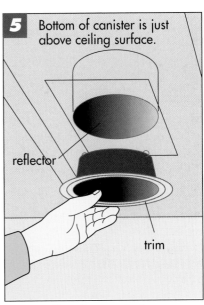

3. Secure the mounting frame.
Slip the mounting frame up through the hole (it will just fit), and place it so the flange sits in the hole. Pull the cable down through the mounting frame. Strip about 6 inches of sheathing from the cable and about ¾ inch of insulation from each wire.

4. Wire the fixture.
Remove the cover plate from the fixture's electrical box. Secure the cable to the box, and connect the wires in the box. Follow the same procedures as if wiring a regular box—see pages 31 and 39. Push the wires into the box and replace the cover plate.

5. Install canister and trim.
Slide the canister up through the mounting plate until it is slightly recessed above the surface of the ceiling. Secure it to the mounting plate by tightening the screws provided. Attach the reflector. Screw in a lightbulb, and attach the trim.

Another configuration
There are several types of recessed lights, all with their own ways of connecting to the ceiling. Here is one that works well if you have access to the space above your ceiling. Once the fixture is positioned over the hole, sliding brackets attached to the canister extend out to reach joists on either side. When these brackets are secured to the joists, the unit is more firmly attached than most recessed fixtures. As with all recessed fixtures, it comes with its own electrical box.

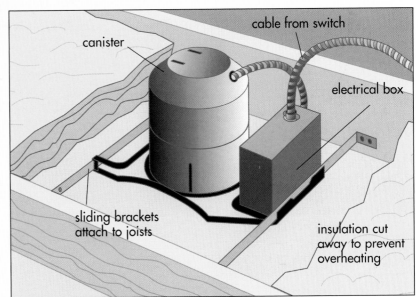

Installing this type
Pound a nail up through the ceiling at the point where you want the light. Go into the space above, find the nail, cut back the insulation, and cut a hole. Install the reflector in the canister. Set the canister in the hole, slide out the brackets, and attach to the joists with nails or general-purpose screws. Wire the box, screw in a bulb, and attach trim.

ADDING WALL SCONCES

Wall sconces are ideal for hallways, stairways, and any room that needs indirect accent lighting. Installing a wall sconce is similar to adding a new light fixture. The only difference is location and the type of fixture box used. As with ceiling lights, you can control as many lights as you want with one switch, or control one or more of them from two different locations by using three-way switches. See pages 84–90 for the various options.

It's ideal if you can secure the fixture box to a framing member as well as the drywall or plaster. Use one of the standard retrofit boxes shown on page 21.

YOU'LL NEED...

TIME: About a full day to install a new switch and two sconces, not including any wall patching.
SKILLS: Basic electrical skills, plus cutting and patching walls.
TOOLS: Keyhole saw, screwdriver, lineman's pliers, drill, fish tape.

Place sconces the same distance up from the floor.

power source

1. Cut holes and run cable.
NOTE: *Shut off the power.* Find a junction box or a receptacle with power you can use. Cut a vertical hole for the switch box and horizontal holes for the sconce boxes (see page 26). Run cable from the power source to the switch and from the switch to the openings cut in the wall for the sconces (see page 32).

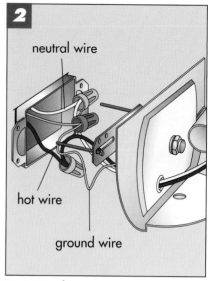

neutral wire

hot wire

ground wire

2. Wire the sconces.
Fasten cable to the boxes, allowing an extra 8 inches of cable to protrude at each box. Attach the boxes to the walls. Strip the sheathing and the wire insulation, and make the electrical connections (see page 31). Note that wires travel both into and out of the first sconce fixture box. Wire the switch (see page 84).

EXPERTS' INSIGHT

THE USES OF SCONCE LIGHTING

■ Wall sconces provide a splash of indirect light that creates the illusion that a room is larger than it is. For this reason, and because they are commonly placed slightly higher than eye level, keep the bulb wattage low.
■ In most cases, wall sconces work best in conjunction with other lights rather than as the primary light source for a room. They work well for ambient light

but are insufficient for specific tasks, such as reading.
■ Install sconces 72 to 78 inches high. Any lower, and you will bump into them; any higher, and they will seem designed to light the ceiling rather than the room.
■ Typically, it makes the most sense to add wall sconces to one wall where accent or indirect lighting is called for. A few sconces go a long way, so keep them spaced more than 6 feet from each other.

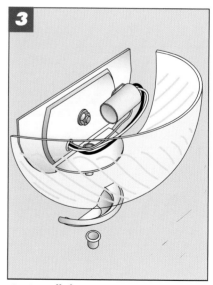

3. Install the sconces.
Tuck the wires into the box, screw a mounting strap to the box, and attach the sconce to the mounting strap. Secure the switch and its cover plate, and test.

INSTALLING UNDER-CABINET LIGHTING

A kitchen is a brighter, more pleasant place to work when its countertops are illuminated by under-cabinet fixtures. Under-cabinet lighting provides a sparkling decorative effect and gives you excellent task lighting.

A 120-volt system requires hours of fishing and installing fixture boxes in one of the most crowded and complicated areas of the house. An attractive alternative is the low-voltage system shown here. Low-voltage halogen lights operated with a remote-controlled, surface-mounted switch can be installed in a day and look as good as a more permanent system.

YOU'LL NEED...

TIME: About a day to install a switch and 10 lights.
SKILLS: Stripping and connecting wires, simple carpentry skills.
TOOLS: Screwdriver, drill, lineman's pliers, keyhole saw.

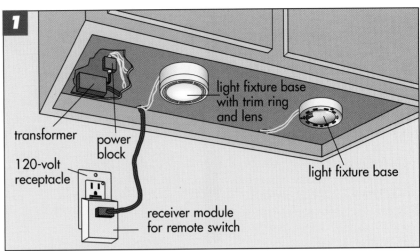

1. Install lights and transformer.
Determine a location for each light fixture where it won't shine in your eyes as you work. Also, halogen lights can be safely attached to wooden cabinets but get hot and should be kept away from plastic and paper goods. Remove the trim ring and lens from each fixture base and attach them with screws to the underside of the cabinets. Align them so the bulbs are the same direction. (Be sure the screws are the right length so they do not poke up into your cabinet.) Drill small holes to allow the wires to pass into your cabinet, and plug their ends into the power block located inside the cabinet. Coil excess wire inside the cabinet. Connect the power block to the transformer. Drill a hole and run a wire from the transformer to a 120-volt receptacle.

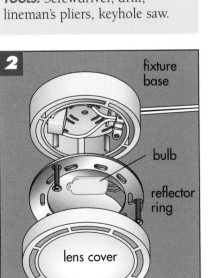

2. Assemble the lights.
Once the fixture bases are installed, snap the lens cover onto the reflector ring. Some under-cabinet lighting kits come with a warning label to attach inside the cabinet door to caution users about the heat of the units.

3. Install the switch.
The switch operates by battery power, so it can be installed anywhere in the kitchen and requires no wiring. Attach the switch housing by screwing it to the wall—use plastic anchors if you can't find a stud. Screw the cover plate to the switch housing.

EXPERTS' INSIGHT

FLUORESCENT UNDER-CABINET LIGHTING

The low-voltage halogen lighting shown here is a convenient improvement when cabinets are already installed. If you are in the process of installing cabinets, consider installing thin (1- to 1½-inch thick) fluorescent lights under the cabinets. To install fluorescent lights, run standard electrical cable behind the walls. Run wires behind the cabinets if possible so you won't have to patch the walls. Or, use raceway wiring attached to the underside of the cabinets (see pages 78–79).

INSTALLING SPECIAL SWITCHES

One of the easiest ways to enhance your home's electrical system is to install special switches. Wiring them is rarely much more difficult than installing a standard switch.

Choose from a wide variety of options. The single-pole dimmer (shown at right), for instance, is touch-sensitive, like a modern elevator button. Touching its flush plate turns lights on and off. Holding a finger on it adjusts the light level. Even that minimal effort isn't necessary with the motion-sensitive switch. It turns on a light fixture whenever someone enters a room then stays on for a prescribed amount of time.

Be aware that some switches have limitations. For example, an ordinary dimmer can only handle up to 600 watts, so it may not be able to operate a chandelier. For higher-wattage fixtures, buy special dimmers able to handle 800, 1,000, or 1,500 watts. (For more information on these and other switches, see pages 16–17.)

If you have ground wires, they all should be connected together in the box, no matter what kind of switch you are installing.

NOTE: *Shut off the power before installing the switch.*

YOU'LL NEED...

TIME: To install most of the switches on these two pages, about an hour.
SKILLS: Connecting wires.
TOOLS: Screwdriver, lineman's pliers, wire stripper.
MATERIALS: Wire connectors, wire for pigtails, electrical tape.

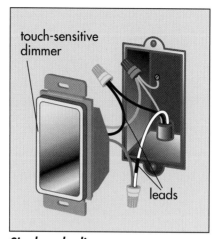

Single-pole dimmer

Most dimmers have a set of leads, or short wires, instead of screw terminals. Hook up a single-pole dimmer as shown.

Most dimmers are deeper than conventional switches, so you may have to rearrange wires in the box before you can fit one in. Don't force dimmers, because they crack easily. If there are too many wires, order a thin-profile unit.

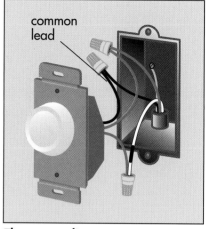

Three-way dimmer

Three-way dimmers have three hot leads. Before you remove the old switch, determine which is the common terminal—it will be printed on the switch body, and/or the screw will be darker-colored than the others. Hook the common wire to the new switch's common lead, and connect the other wires. (For more on three-way switches, see pages 87–88.)

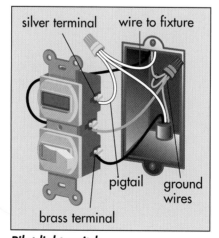

Pilot-light switch

This switch has a bulb that glows when its fixture is on. Connect the black feed wire to the brass terminal on the side that does not have a connecting tab. Pigtail two white wires, and connect them to the silver terminal. Connect the black wire that leads to the fixture to the terminal on the side with the connecting tab.

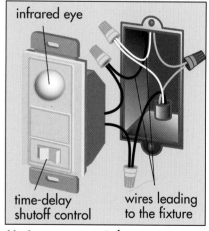

Motion-sensor switch

An infrared beam detects movement and turns on a light fixture. A time-delay feature lets you choose how long the light remains on. Connect the neutral wires to each other, not to the switch. Connect the black feed wire to one lead. To the other lead, attach the black wire that runs to the fixture.

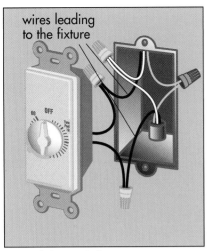

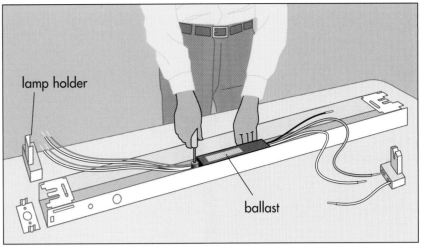

Time-delay switch

With this type of switch, you turn a spring-driven dial to set the switch so it will turn off a fixture after a delay ranging from 1 to 60 minutes. Connect the black leads to the black wires in the box, and connect the white wires together, not to the switch.

Fluorescent dimmer

Fluorescent dimmer switches connect in the same way as incandescent dimmers (see page 74), but you must equip each lamp with a special ballast. Remove the fixture. Mark the wires with pieces of tape so you'll know where to refasten them. Remove the lamp holders and disconnect their wires by poking

into the terminals with a nail or thin screwdriver. Remove the old ballast and install a new dimming ballast. Reconnect the lamp holders. Reinstall the fluorescent fixture. If more than one fluorescent light is connected to a dimmer switch, all the bulbs must be the same size and share the same ballast (for replacing a ballast, see page 55).

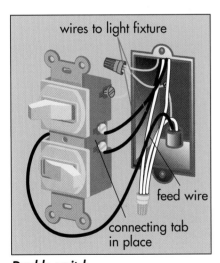

Double switch

This unit has two switches that fit into a single-switch space. Attach the feed wire to a terminal on the side with the connecting tab. (This tab enables the wire to supply power to both switches.) Connect the two wires that lead to the two fixtures to the terminals on the other side, and connect the white wires together, not to the switch.

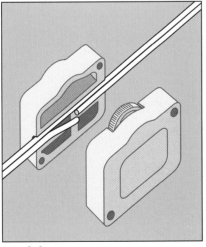

Cord dimmer

You can purchase in-line cord dimmers for lamps that do not have switches. Some, such as this one, automatically pierce the insulation when you put the unit together. Others require stripping the wires before assembling.

Money $ Saver

These switches not only give you greater control over your lighting but can save money as well: A dimmer switch enables you to operate a bulb at less than its full intensity so you save energy and prolong the life of the bulb. Time-delay and pilot-light switches keep you from burning lights unnecessarily. Programmable switches (see page 17) save money and provide security while you are on vacation. You can program them to turn lights on and off in a pattern that makes it appear you are still at home.

CHOOSING GFCI RECEPTACLES, BREAKERS

Fuses and circuit breakers protect the wiring in your home. A ground-fault circuit interrupter (GFCI) protects people who might otherwise get a dangerous shock.

A GFCI has a microprocessor that senses tiny leakages of current and shuts off the power instantly. In most circumstances, leakage of current isn't a big problem. In properly grounded systems most of it is carried back to the service panel. What remains would scarcely give you a tickle. But if you are well grounded—standing on a wet lawn or touching a plumbing component, for example—that tiny bit of current would pass through your body on its way to the earth. As little as $\frac{1}{5}$ of an amp, just enough to light a 25-watt bulb, can be dangerous.

A GFCI is wired into both wires of a circuit so it can continuously compare current levels flowing through the hot and neutral sides. These should always be equal. If the microprocessor senses a difference of just $\frac{1}{200}$ of an amp, it almost instantly trips the circuit.

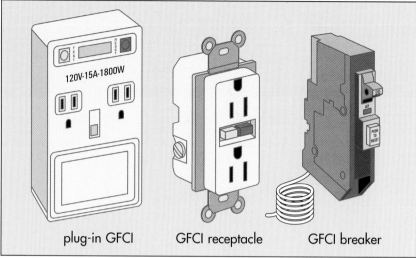

plug-in GFCI　　GFCI receptacle　　GFCI breaker

120V-15A-1800W

Power is interrupted in $\frac{1}{40}$ of a second or less, cutting off the power before you're seriously hurt. Any ground fault is a potential hazard. If a tool or appliance is faulty, it can give you a serious shock even if its grounding wire is in good condition. So GFCI protection is a good idea anywhere you might be in contact with water while using electricity.

There are three types of GFCIs: plug-ins, receptacles, and breakers. To install a portable plug-in unit, simply insert its blades into a

receptacle and plug in the appliance. A GFCI receptacle replaces a conventional receptacle, and properly placed can protect other receptacles on the same circuit. Install a GFCI breaker into a service panel to protect a circuit.

YOU'LL NEED...

TIME: To install either a receptacle or a breaker, 1 to 2 hours.
SKILLS: Connecting wires.
TOOLS: Screwdriver, wire stripper, lineman's pliers.

Electrical codes require GFCI receptacles in the places where you're likely to ground an

electrical appliance. In a kitchen, GFCIs often are required for all receptacles within 6 feet of a

sink. All bathroom receptacles, as well as all outdoor receptacles, must be GFCI-protected.

INSTALLING GFCI DEVICES

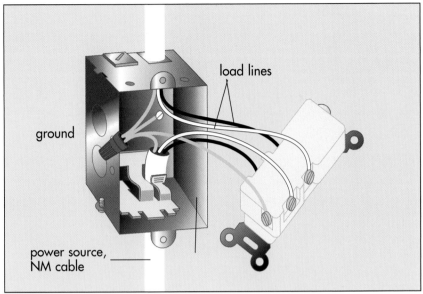

Wire a GFCI receptacle.
Attach a GFCI receptacle as shown above, connecting multiple wires with pigtails. Incoming power goes to the line leads or terminals. Load lines carry it to other receptacles on the circuit. So if you install a GFCI in the first receptacle of a circuit, the entire circuit will be protected. If you are installing a GFCI at the end of a line, cap off the load leads with wire connectors, or buy a version that protects only one receptacle.

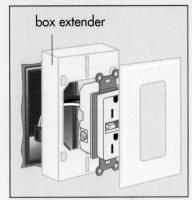
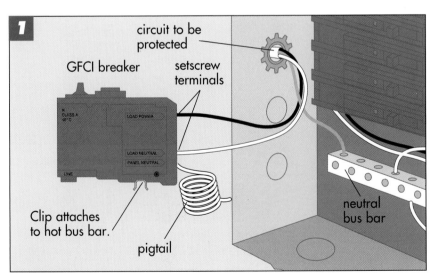

1. To install a GFCI breaker, connect hot and neutral wires.
You can clip a GFCI breaker into a service panel as you would an ordinary breaker (see page 107), but you must wire it differently. **NOTE:** *Shut off the power.* Shut off the main breaker and be careful not to touch the hot wires coming into the box (see pages 106–107). Select the circuit you wish to protect, unclip the old breaker from the hot bus bar, and slip it out of the service panel. Disconnect the hot and neutral wires from the old breaker. Attach both wires to the setscrew terminals of the new GFCI breaker as shown. Strip half an inch of insulation from the pigtail.

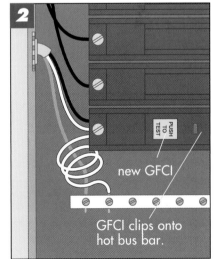

2. Ground and install the breaker.
Loosen a terminal on the neutral bus bar, and connect the white pigtail by inserting the wire and tightening the screw. Clipping the GFCI breaker into place attaches it to the hot bus bar. Turn the power back on, set the breaker, and push the test button. The breaker should trip.

ADDING SURFACE-MOUNTED WIRING

If you do not want to cut into your walls, fish wires, and patch and paint afterward, consider surface-mounted wiring, often called "raceway" wiring. Surface-mounted components are available in metal or plastic and are comparatively easy to install. The system's main drawback is the way it looks. But for informal settings—a basement or a work room, for instance—it is a convenient alternative.

NOTE: *Shut off the power before tying into existing receptacles.*

YOU'LL NEED...
TIME: For a system like the one shown, about 4 hours.
SKILLS: Connecting wires, measuring and cutting the components.
TOOLS: Hacksaw and miter box, basic electrician's tools.

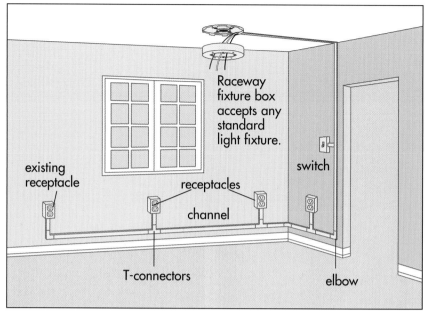

Raceway fixture box accepts any standard light fixture.

existing receptacle

switch

receptacles

channel

T-connectors

elbow

Plan the job.
Check your local codes. They probably limit raceway wiring to dry locations where the walls are not subject to damage (as they are, for example, in a garage). Decide where you want the pieces to go, and measure carefully for all the runs. Take your calculations to your electrical supplier and have a salesperson help you choose the parts you need.

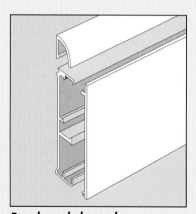

Baseboard channel
Decorative and functional plastic baseboard channel can be added onto existing baseboard or even substituted for it. This type of channel is designed to simultaneously carry household wiring, coaxial cable, and telephone and computer lines. Extension boxes with receptacles, phone jacks, and coaxial hookups can be added at various points along its length.

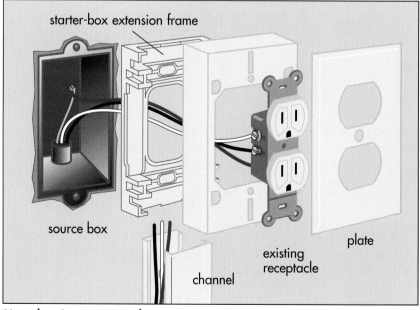

starter-box extension frame

source box

channel

existing receptacle

plate

How the pieces go together
A raceway system begins by tapping into an existing circuit at a receptacle by using a "starter box." This extends the existing outlet so it can match up with the wall-mounted channel. Twist-away holes allow you to exit the box with raceway channel from any direction. Additional receptacles—as well as switches and light fixtures—mount directly on the wall. Begin by selecting a receptacle on a circuit that has enough capacity for additional outlets (see page 12).

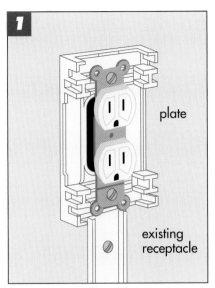

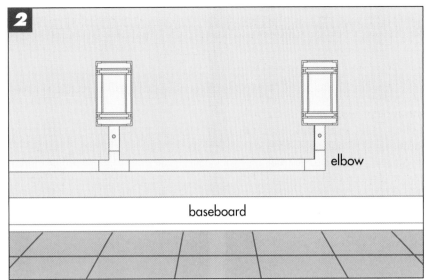

elbow

baseboard

1. Start at the box.

NOTE: *Shut off the power.* Remove the receptacle and install the starter box, onto which the receptacle will be reinstalled as shown. Map out the system from this starting point.

2. Cut and assemble components.

When you measure the channel sections for cutting, take into account the elbows, Ts, and other connectors. Cut the channels with a hacksaw and a miter box. Use extension connectors to tie the ends of channels together, and Ts and elbows at corners. Measure carefully from the floor, and use a level to make sure the receptacles are at the same height.

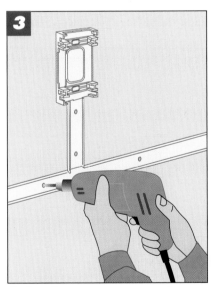

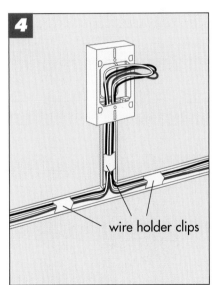

wire holder clips

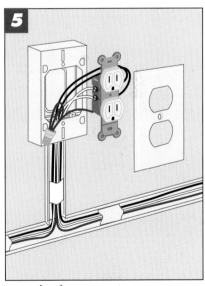

3. Attach components securely.

The channels will be bumped by furniture and normal household traffic, so take care to attach them securely. Locate studs and drill screws into them where possible. Use plastic anchors for places where you can't reach studs.

4. Run the wires.

Run the wiring and hold it in place every foot or so with specially designed clips. Be sure to leave 6–8 inches of wire at each outlet so you will have room to strip and make connections.

5. Make the connections.

Connect all fixtures and receptacles (see pages 28–31). Connect to the existing receptacle, turn the power back on, and test the new fixtures and receptacles. Install the snap-on covers for the channels, fittings, and boxes.

INSTALLING CEILING FANS

Whether it's keeping warm air down for heat in the winter, or circulating cool air in the summer, a ceiling fan can cut energy costs and help keep your home more comfortable all year long. Installing a ceiling fan is an ideal one-day project for homeowners with little or no wiring experience. Most fans have pull switches that turn the unit off and on, and control fan speed. You can also install wall switches to control the fan (see page 84).

YOU'LL NEED...

TIME: About 4 to 6 hours if you need to run new wiring.
SKILLS: Simple carpentry and wiring skills.
TOOLS: Screwdriver, utility knife, keyhole saw, wrench, socket driver, needle-nose pliers.

HOW TO CHOOSE A FAN, CEILING BOX, AND BRACE BAR

You'll have many different types of ceiling boxes and brace bars to choose from at your local hardware store or home center. Some are variations on the fan brace bar shown on these pages. Others are reinforced plastic or thick-gauge metal fixture boxes designed to support fans.

The types worth purchasing have two features in common: They are extra strong, and they attach by some means directly to the ceiling joists. Never install a fan bracket or fixture box that is supported only by the ceiling material.

If you have access from above, you can add in framing to support a heavy-duty ceiling box attached with general-purpose screws.

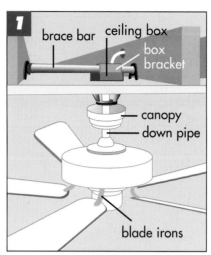

1. Select a brace bar.
If you don't have access from above, you'll need a ceiling fan support, known as a brace bar, which can be inserted from the room below. Typically, it consists of an adjustable bar installed between two joists.

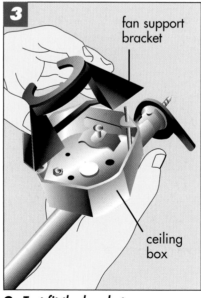

3. Test-fit the bracket.
Check that the fan support bracket fits and can be attached easily once the box is in place. Push out a ceiling box knockout (a tab covering a hole in the back or one of the sides), and install a cable clamp. Disassemble the brace bar, ceiling box, and box bracket.

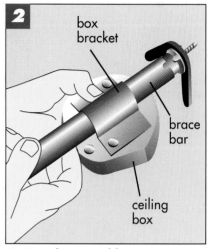

2. Test the assembly.
Do a dry run of assembling the brace bar, ceiling box, and box bracket. Be sure you fully understand how the brace bar is fastened in place and how the box is attached. Follow the instructions that come with it. Once installed, these items are hard to remove.

CEILING FAN CLEARANCES AND CAPACITY

For safety—and to give the fan adequate space to effectively move air—use the clearances shown below. Select fan blades to suit the square footage of the room.

Fan Diameter (inches)	Room Area (square feet)
36	96
42	144
48	288
52	400

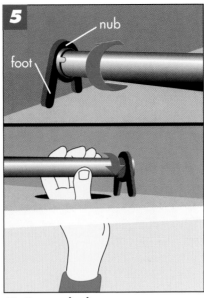

4. Position brace bar.
Cut a hole in the ceiling about 5 inches in diameter (see pages 26–27 for tips on locating it). Most brace bars have a screwlike fastener at each end that fixes the bar in place. Tip the bar through the hole, then center it over the hole, perpendicular to the joists.

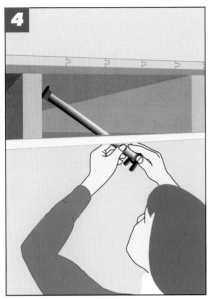

5. Fasten the bar.
Turn the outermost piece of the brace bar until it locks into the nub. Continue turning until the first foot is fastened. Next, turn the innermost bar to fasten the other foot.

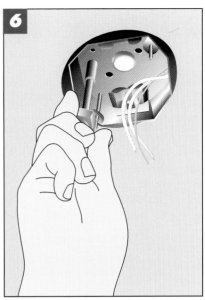

6. Attach the box.
Pull wires into the receptacle box. Loosely fasten one side of box bracket, and position the bracket on the brace bar. Feed the second bracket bolt through the box, and fasten nuts on both of the bolts using a socket driver or pliers.

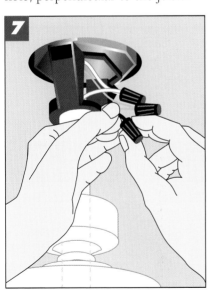

7. Wire the fan.
Attach the fan support bracket and the down pipe. Connect the fan leads to the circuit wires using wire connectors. Simply attach white to white, black to black, and the ground wires to the green lead. Manufacturers usually provide instructions. Wire the fan following the instructions.

EXPERTS' INSIGHT

Balancing a wobbly fan

All may not be gentle breezes when you turn on your fan. Particularly at high speed, it may rock and roll. Don't panic. It might not be a manufacturer's defect or the result of shoddy installation. It's more likely that the fan blades need balancing. Buy an inexpensive ceiling fan balancing kit, and follow its simple procedures for checking the blades. If the problem persists, try the following.

■ Check for any loose screws where the blades attach to the blade irons (the supports that radiate from the motor shaft).

■ Remove the fan blades, and lay them on a flat surface to check that they are not warped. If one is warped, ask your retailer to replace the entire set.

■ Check the blade irons. They are typically set at a 12-degree angle, though on small fans they can be pitched as high as 25 degrees. Remove the irons and set them on top of each other. If one doesn't match the others, replace it.

■ With the blades and blade irons removed, run the fan motor at its highest speed. The shaft should not wobble. If it does, the motor is defective.

INSTALLING TELEPHONE AND CABLE LINES

The telephone and cable companies will install cable for you, but be braced for a pretty hefty bill, even for running a simple surface-mounted extension line. The cable company may want to charge you a monthly fee for splitting the line in order to service two televisions. So, although it is not feasible for a homeowner to make major telephone installations (and perhaps illegal to make a cable installation), it does make sense for you to run cable for extra telephones or a second TV.

You'll find that running wires for telephones and cable TV is easier than electrical wiring. There is no danger of shock, and only one cable to run. Still, the same principles of installation and connection apply: You must protect wire insulation from damage and be sure connections are secure.

The simplest way to install the cable is to tack or staple it to the wall. Although a common practice, this can be unsightly and a mess when you paint walls and molding. For a neater and more permanent installation, take the time to run the cable out of sight.

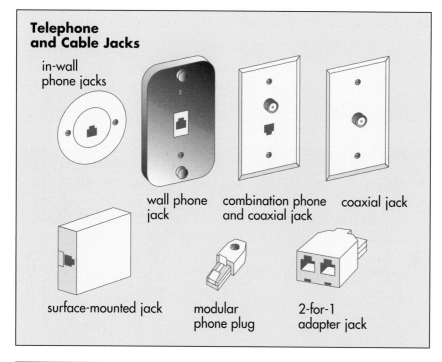

Telephone and Cable Jacks

in-wall phone jacks

wall phone jack

combination phone and coaxial jack

coaxial jack

surface-mounted jack

modular phone plug

2-for-1 adapter jack

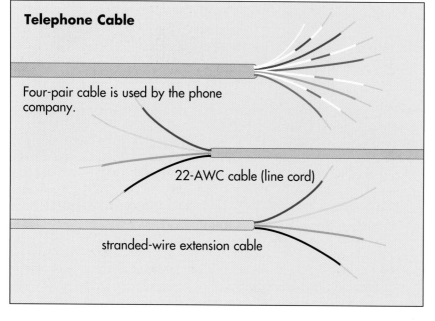

Telephone Cable

Four-pair cable is used by the phone company.

22-AWC cable (line cord)

stranded-wire extension cable

YOU'LL NEED...

TIME: Several hours for a typical extension of a television cable or telephone line.
SKILLS: Connecting wires, possibly some carpentry skills.
TOOLS: Drill, screwdriver, pliers, wire stripper, carpentry tools.

EXPERTS' INSIGHT

THE RIGHT CABLE

■ To avoid a noisy connection and possible damage to your phone system, use cable marked 22-AWC (often sold as "line cord") to add a branch line. Stranded-wire extension cable sold in 25- and 50-foot lengths, it should only be used between the jack and the phone, not for adding new extensions. This solid-core cable is more expensive than stranded wires or (the worst of all) filament wire, but well worth the investment.
■ Purchase shielded coaxial cable for television cables. It has a metal wrapping under the insulation. Nonshielded cable will not perform as well.

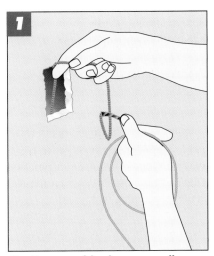

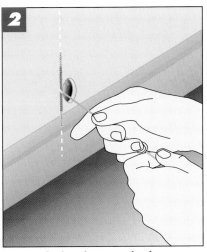

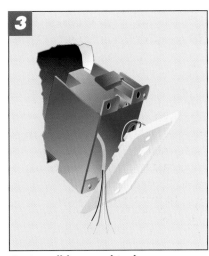

1. To run cable down a wall, attach to a chain and drop down.
Cut a hole in the wall where you want to locate an in-wall phone or cable jack. Attach a length of beaded chain to the end of the cable with electrician's tape. Drop the chain down through the hole. If you feel it hitting an obstruction, give it a wiggle.

2. Grab the chain at the bottom.
Once the chain has dropped far enough, drill a hole in the wall at the point where you want to retrieve the cable. (To hide the cable completely, remove the baseboard molding first.) Insert a bent piece of coat hanger wire, and root around until you hook the chain. Pull the chain through the hole until a foot or so of cable is sticking out.

3. Install box and jack.
Where you want a new phone or coaxial cable jack, cut out the wall as you would for an electrical box (see page 26). Pull about 8 inches of cable through the box. Install the box. For phone cable, strip the sheathing and insulation, and make connections as marked on the jack. At the phone junction box, connect the wires to the color-coded terminals. (For coaxial cable connections, see below.)

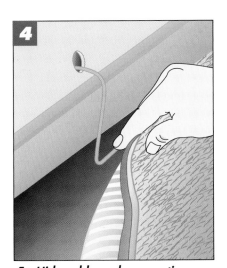

4. Hide cable under carpeting.
If you don't want to go to the trouble of pulling up your baseboard, it is often possible to hide most of the cable under wall-to-wall carpeting. Pry up only two feet or so of carpeting at a time, or you may have trouble getting it to reattach to the tack strip. Slip the cable in place, and push the carpet firmly back in place as you go.

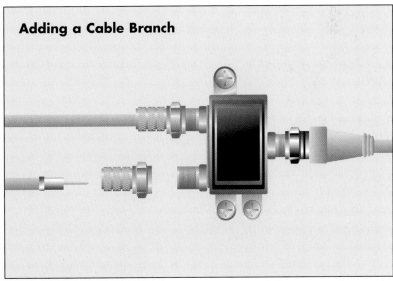

Adding a Cable Branch

Make coaxial connections.
To hook an additional television to your cable, add a two-way splitter. Mount the splitter to a wall, floor, or baseboard and run cable. Add a screw-on connector to both ends of the cable by stripping ¾ inch of insulation (cutting all the way to the wire), taking care not to bend the wire. Next strip ⅜ inch of the thin outer insulation only, leaving the metal wrapping intact. Screw the connector on—it will grab the insulation firmly. Attach the connector to the splitter.

WIRING CEILING FIXTURES WITH SWITCHES

*D*epending on which way is easier to run cable, you can wire a ceiling fixture with the power coming into the box (as on this page), or with power coming into the switch (as on page 85).

Here, as with the configurations on the following six pages, the type of fixture doesn't matter. Whether it is a flush-mounted light, track lighting, a chandelier, or a ceiling fan, the rough wiring to the fixture is the same.

YOU'LL NEED...
TIME: Not including running the cable and installing boxes, about an hour making connections.
SKILLS: Basic electrical skills.
TOOLS: Lineman's pliers, screwdriver, wire stripper, cable ripper, side-cutting pliers or combination tool.

power source

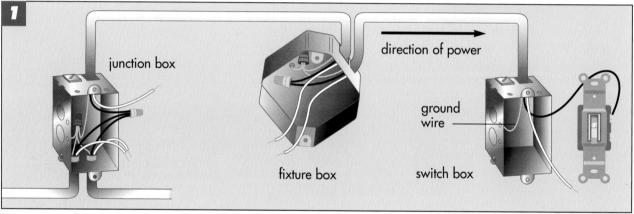

junction box

direction of power

ground wire

fixture box   switch box

1. Begin making connections.
NOTE: *Shut off power.* Install fixture and switch box, if they do not already exist (see pages 24–25). Find a junction box that has power from a circuit you can use. Run two-wire cable from the junction box to the fixture box, and from the fixture box to the switch. Connect the ground wires as shown. Connect all the black wires as shown. Note how the black wire picks up power at the junction box and carries it to the fixture box then on to the switch.

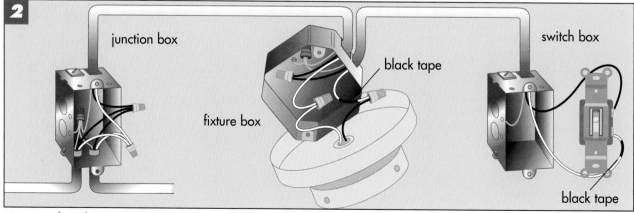

junction box

switch box

black tape

fixture box

black tape

2. Complete the connections.
Mark the white wire running from the switch box to the fixture box with black tape on both ends. Attach one end to the switch. At the fixture box, connect the black-taped white wire to the black fixture wire, and the untaped white wire to the white fixture wire. At the junction box, connect all white wires together. (For how to connect wires, see page 31.)

WIRING TWO CEILING FIXTURES

In this wiring configuration, power comes to the switch first, then goes to both of the fixtures. (A single light also can be wired this way.) A single switch can control many fixtures. Just extend the run from one to the next. If you have multiple fixtures on a single line, make sure the wattage or amperage total of fixtures on the line doesn't exceed the maximum indicated on the body of the switch.

YOU'LL NEED...

TIME: Not including running the cable and installing boxes, about 1½ hours to plan and complete the connections.
SKILLS: Basic electrical skills.
TOOLS: Lineman's pliers, needle-nose pliers, wire stripper, cable ripper, screwdriver, side-cutting pliers or combination tool.

power source

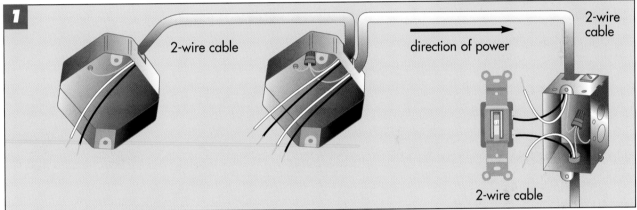

2-wire cable

direction of power

2-wire cable

2-wire cable

1. Begin making connections.
NOTE: *Shut off power.* Install fixture boxes and a switch box, if they do not already exist (see pages 24–25). Find a junction box that has power from a circuit you can use. Run two-wire cable from the junction box to the fixture box (see pages 32-35 for instructions on running cable), and from the fixture box to the next fixture box. Connect the ground wires as shown (see page 31). At the switch box, hook both black wires to the terminals. The current in the black wires passes through the switch so the switch can allow it to flow (on) or stop the flow (off).

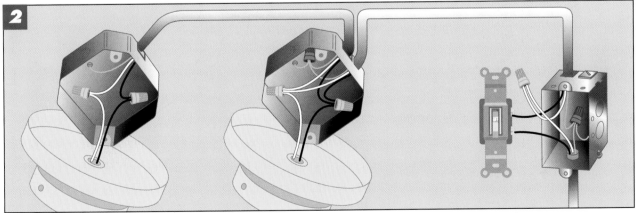

2. Complete the connections.
At the switch box, connect the two white wires together. At the first fixture box, connect all three black wires together, and connect all three white wires together. At the second fixture box, connect the black wires together, and connect the white wires together.

Note that you also can control two or more fixtures with the power coming to the fixture, but it's more complicated. Route the power as on page 84, and connect the second fixture's black wire to the black-taped white wire in the first fixture box. (For how to connect wires, see page 31.)

WIRING FIXTURES WITH SEPARATE SWITCHES

If you are installing ceiling fixtures and a switch box, with a little more work, you can provide individual switches for the fixtures. Use a two-gang box for the switches, and run three-wire cable between the fixtures and to the switch. Power comes to the fixtures by means of two-wire cable. Electricians are fond of three-wire cable because in many instances it allows you to run one cable instead of two.

YOU'LL NEED...
TIME: Not including running the cable and installing boxes, about 1½ hours to make connections.
SKILLS: Basic electrical skills.
TOOLS: Lineman's pliers, cable ripper, screwdriver, wire stripper, needle-nose pliers, side-cutting pliers or combination tool.

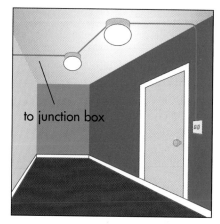
to junction box

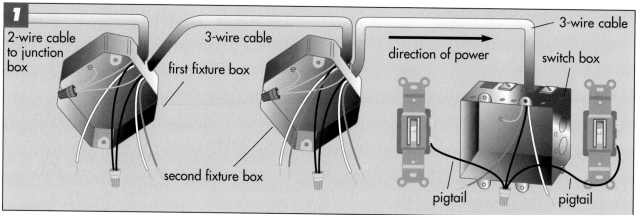

1. Begin making connections.
NOTE: *Shut off power.* Install fixture boxes and a switch box, if they do not already exist (see pages 24–25). Run two-wire cable from a junction box to the first

fixture box. Run three-wire cable from the first to the second fixture box, and from there to the switch box. Connect all ground wires as shown, using green connectors. Bring power to the switches by

connecting the black wires in all three boxes, as shown. In the switch box, cut pigtails (the two short pieces of wire), and connect them to the switches.

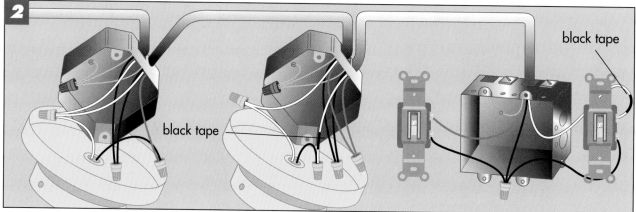

2. Complete the connections.
At the switch box, connect the red wire to a switch and the white wire to the other switch. Wrap black tape on the white wire, both at the switch box and at the fixture

box to show that it is hot. At the second fixture box, connect the two red wires together. At both fixture boxes, connect the hot and neutral wires to the fixture wires, as shown. Or install this wiring

configuration with power coming to the switch. Split the incoming black wire, and run the outgoing red and black wires to the fixtures. The neutral white wire, shared by both switches, passes on through.

WIRING THREE-WAY SWITCHES

*T*hree-way switches control power to a fixture from two separate points, allowing you to control a ceiling light from either side of a room. Three-way switches use a three-wire system, composed of a power wire and two interconnecting wires called travelers. Unless you have metal conduit or armored cable, you also need a fourth, grounding wire. Power comes in through one switch, travels to the fixture and to the second switch (see page 89 for the ABCs of three-way switching).

YOU'LL NEED...
TIME: Not including running the cable and installing boxes, about 1½ hours to make connections.
SKILLS: Basic electrical skills.
TOOLS: Lineman's pliers, wire stripper, cable ripper, needle-nose pliers, side-cutting pliers, screwdriver.

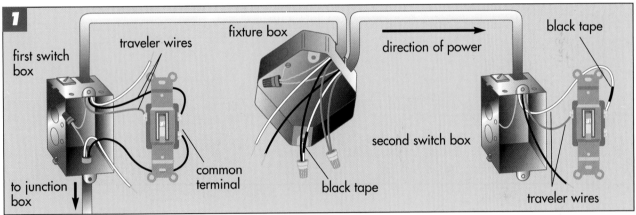

1. Begin making connections.
NOTE: *Shut off power.* Install switch boxes and a fixture box (see pages 24–25). Run two-wire cable from a junction box to the first switch box. Run three-wire cable from the first switch box to the fixture box, and from the fixture box to the second switch box. Connect all ground wires as shown (for how to connect wires, see page 31). At the first switch box, connect the hot wire to the common terminal on the switch (it is labeled and/or is darker than the other two). Attach traveler wires to the other two terminals.

At the second switch box, attach the red and white wires to the noncommon terminals of the switch. Wrap a piece of black tape on the white wire, both here and at the fixture box. At the fixture box, connect the two red wires, and connect the marked white wire to the black wire that comes from the first switch.

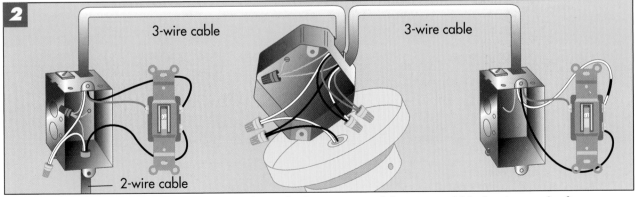

2. Complete the connections.
At the second switch box, connect the black wire to the common terminal on the switch. This completes the hot portion of the circuit. At the first switch box, connect the two white wires. At the fixture box, connect the white and black wires to the fixture. Once completed, either switch will operate the light.

WIRING THREE-WAYS, POWER TO SWITCH

Page 87 shows how to wire three-way switches when the light is between two switches. Here we show the light beyond both switches. We've included a dimmer in this example. (With most dimmers, you can use only one per circuit.)

For this configuration, you run three-wire cable only between the switches. Power comes into the first switch and out of the second on just two wires.

YOU'LL NEED...
TIME: Not including running the cable and installing boxes, about 1½ hours to make the connections.
SKILLS: Basic electrical skills.
TOOLS: Lineman's pliers, cable ripper, screwdriver, wire stripper, needle-nose pliers, side-cutting pliers or combination tool.

power source

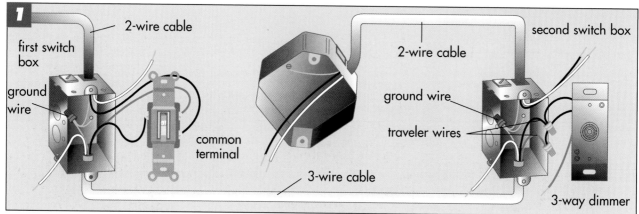

1. Begin making connections.
NOTE: *Shut off power.* Install switch boxes and a fixture box (see pages 24–25). Run two-wire cable from a junction box to the first switch box. Run three-wire cable from the first switch box to the second, and two-wire cable from the second switch box to the fixture box (see pages 32–35). Connect ground wires as shown. At the first switch box, connect the black (hot) wire of the power source to the switch's common terminal (see page 31). Connect traveler wires to the other terminals. At the second switch box, connect the travelers. (Note: A three-way dimmer can burn out if hooked up incorrectly. Check by setting up the circuit with ordinary three-way switches and turning on the power. Then replace one switch with a dimmer.)

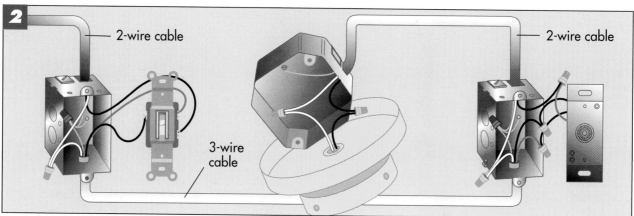

2. Complete the connections.
At the second switch box, connect the black wire that goes to the fixture box with the dimmer's common wire. Connect the two white wires.

At the first switch box, connect the white wires. At the fixture box, connect black to black wires and white to white wires. Install the switches and switch plates and the light fixture.

WIRING THREE-WAYS, POWER TO FIXTURE

In this situation, power comes to the light fixture, then proceeds to the two switches. A two-wire cable runs to the fixture and to the first switch box. A three-wire cable runs only from switch box to switch box.

YOU'LL NEED...

TIME: After running cable and installing boxes, 1½ hours
SKILLS: Basic electrical skills.
TOOLS: See page 88.

ABCs OF THREE-WAYS

Follow these principles when installing any three-way configuration: **A.** Always attach the incoming hot (black) wire to the common terminal of one switch. **B.** Use traveler wires to connect the traveler terminals to each other, never to the light. **C.** Connect the common terminal of the second switch only to the black fixture wire.

power source

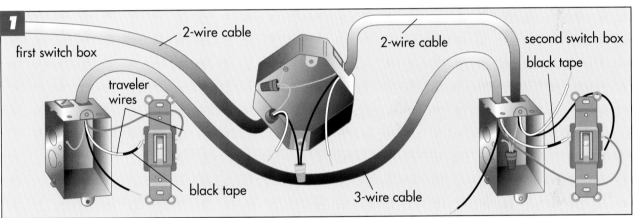

first switch box
2-wire cable
2-wire cable
second switch box
black tape
traveler wires
black tape
3-wire cable

1. Begin making connections.
At the ceiling box, connect the black, hot wires. At the first switch box, connect the hot wire to the common terminal and the traveler wires to the other terminals. Wrap a piece of black tape on either end of the white wire to show that it is hot. At the second switch box, attach the traveler wires.

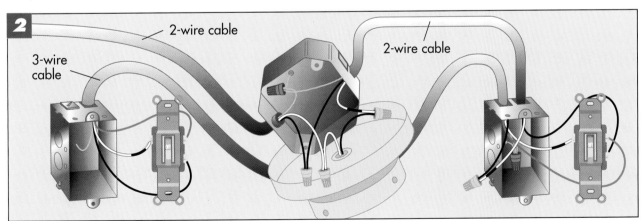

2-wire cable
2-wire cable
3-wire cable

2. Complete the connections.
At the second switch, connect the black wire to the common terminal. At the first switch box, connect the black and white wires, and wrap a piece of black tape at either end of the white wire to show that it is hot. At the fixture box, connect white to white wire and the black-marked white wire to the black wire of the fixture.

WIRING FOUR-WAY SWITCHES

*T*o control a fixture from three or more different switches, use one or more four-way switches. You can install any number of them between a pair of three-way switches. In four-way situations, the first and last switches must always be three-ways.

Here, incoming power flows from switch to switch to switch then to the fixture, but it also could take one of the routes illustrated previously.

YOU'LL NEED...

TIME: Not including running the cable and installing boxes, about 2 hours to make the connections for a fixture and three switches.
SKILLS: Basic electrical skills.
TOOLS: Lineman's pliers, cable ripper, wire stripper, screwdriver, needle-nose pliers, side-cutting pliers or combination tool.

power source

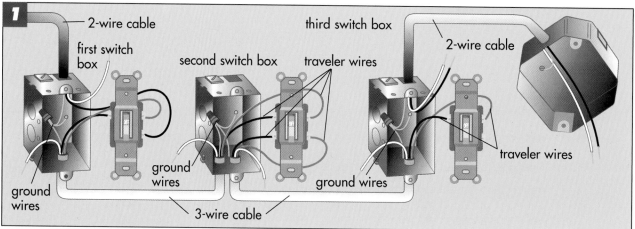

1. **Begin making connections.**
NOTE: *Shut off power.* Install switch boxes and a fixture box. Run two-wire cable from a junction box to the first switch box. Run three-wire cable from the first switch box to the second and third, and two-wire cable from the third switch box to the fixture box. Connect all ground wires.

At the first switch box, connect the black wire from the power source to the switch's common terminal. Connect the traveler wires to the other terminals.

At the second and third switches, connect the traveler wires as shown. The four-way switch carries only traveler wires. (For how to connect wires, see page 31.)

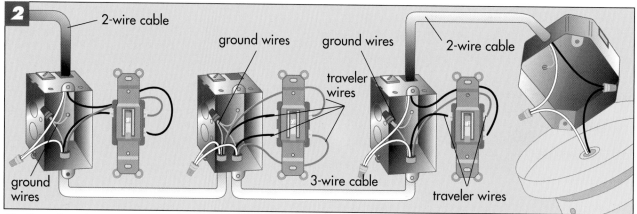

2. **Complete the connections.**
At the third switch, connect the fixture box's black wire to the common terminal. Connect the white wires. Connect the white wires at the first and second switch boxes. Connect the fixture to the two wires at the fixture box and install the switches and switch plates. Once completed, you can turn the fixture on and off from any of the three switches.

ADDING RECEPTACLES

Once you find a usable power source, adding a receptacle is easy to figure out. Most of the work is cutting the wall, installing a box, fishing the cable, and patching the wall.

You can tap into an existing receptacle, as shown on this page, only if it is at the end of a wiring run. If it's in the middle of a run, all of its terminals will be occupied.

YOU'LL NEED...
TIME: Not including running the cable and installing boxes, about an hour to make connections.
SKILLS: Basic electrical skills.
TOOLS: Lineman's pliers, cable ripper, screwdriver, wire stripper, needle-nose pliers, side-cutting pliers or combination tool.

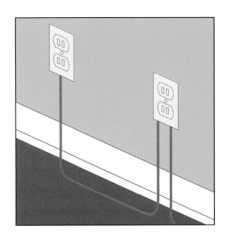

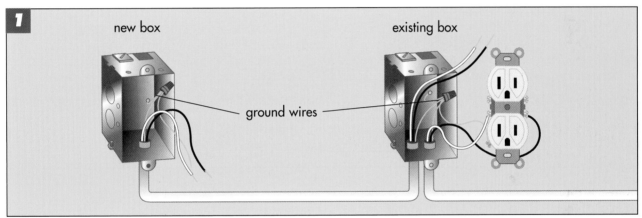

new box   existing box

ground wires

1. Begin making connections.
NOTE: *Shut off power.* Find a receptacle box where you can draw power without overcrowding the box or overloading the circuit. (You also can draw power from a junction box. Just connect to the hot and neutral wires instead of to the receptacle.) Install the new receptacle box. Run a two-wire cable from the existing box to the new box.

Remove the screws that secure the existing receptacle to the box, and pull it out so you can work on it. Connect the ground wires in both boxes as shown.

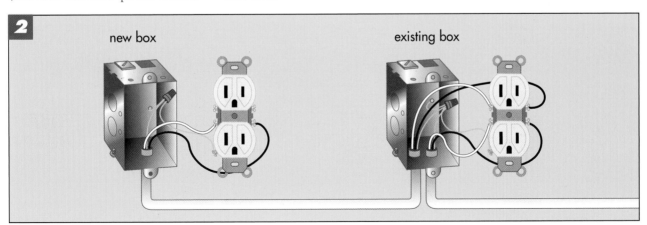

new box   existing box

2. Complete the connections.
At the existing box, connect the black wire to the hot receptacle terminal, which is brass-colored. Connect the white wire to the other terminal. At the new box, also connect the black wire to the hot terminal and the white wire to the other terminal. Wrap both receptacles with electrician's tape so that all the terminals are covered. Fasten both receptacles in place, turn on power and test your installation. Finally, attach the receptacle plates.

ADDING 240-VOLT RECEPTACLES

Some 240-volt equipment—central air-conditioning units and electric water heaters, for example—have no plugs and are wired directly into junction boxes because they do not need to be moved. Ranges, clothes dryers, and other appliances are connected by cords and plugs and require special receptacles.

The wiring requirements for 240-volt circuits are specific. For a 30-amp dryer, use a 30-amp breaker and 10-gauge wire. For a 50-amp range, use a 50-amp breaker and 6-gauge wire. Choose a receptacle designed to provide the correct amperage for your appliance and has holes to match the prongs on the plug.

YOU'LL NEED...

TIME: To install a 240-volt receptacle after the wiring is completed, about an hour.
SKILLS: Running cable, stripping and connecting wires.
TOOLS: Screwdriver, wire stripper, lineman's pliers.

CAUTION!

DANGER! HIGH VOLTAGE!
Wiring for 240-volt receptacles is no different from regular 120 lines, except that the danger is much, much greater. Even if you are dry and are wearing rubber-soled shoes, a jolt of this current could do you serious physical harm and perhaps even kill you. Check and double-check that the power is off before installing a 240-volt receptacle. This is one job where you may want to call in an experienced electrician, just for safety's sake.

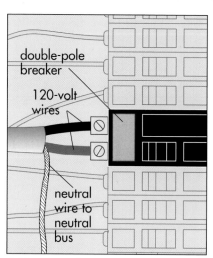

240-volt wiring
NOTE: *Shut off the power.* Wiring starts at a 240-volt breaker or fuse at the service panel and ends at a specially designed receptacle. A 240-volt circuit should supply only one appliance; no other receptacles can be attached to it. Connect 120-volt wires to a breaker and the neutral wire to the neutral bus (see pages 106–107)

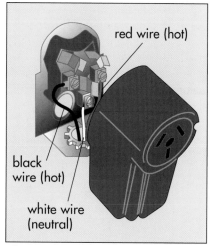

Floor-mounted 240-volt receptacle
If no outlet box is available, you can install this unit on the floor. Position it so it won't get bumped when you move the appliance. Remove the cover, and connect the neutral wire to the terminal marked "white," and the red and black wires to the other terminals. All receptacles shown on this page use the neutral wire as ground.

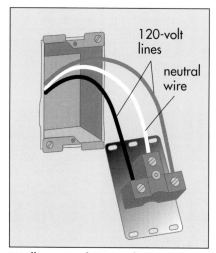

Wall-mounted 240-volt receptacle
Install a receptacle box and run 10-3 cable (for a 30-amp breaker) or 6-3 cable (for a 50-amp breaker) to it. (For information on running cable in finished spaces, see page 32; for information on selecting cable, see page 19.) Strip the black, red, and white wires to the length marked on the receptacle housing and attach.

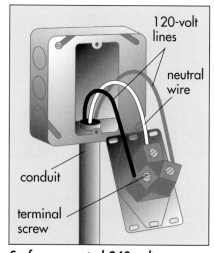

Surface-mounted 240-volt receptacle for basement or garage
Install a box (see pages 24–26) and run conduit (see pages 42–44) to the desired location. Fish red, black, and white 10- or 6-gauge wire (see page 45). Strip wires and insert them into the slots in the terminals as shown; tighten the screws.

SPLITTING, SWITCHING RECEPTACLES

Examine a standard duplex receptacle, and you'll see that each set of terminals on either side is connected by a small metal tab—one silver-colored, one brass-colored. If you break this bridge, the upper and lower receptacles can be used independently, one controlled by a switch and one functioning like a standard receptacle. A split receptacle is handy when you want to turn a living room lamp on and off from a wall switch, for example, but still leave half of the receptacle for general use. Sometimes you may need a split receptacle when you want to supply the two outlets of a heavily used receptacle with two different circuits.

YOU'LL NEED...
TIME: With the cables and boxes in place, about an hour to make the connections.
SKILLS: Basic electrical skills.
TOOLS: Screwdriver, wire strippers, lineman's pliers, needle-nose pliers

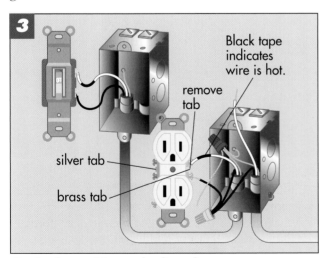

1. Install cable and boxes.
NOTE: *Shut off the power.* Disconnect the receptacle and run two-wire cable to a switch box. Hook up the ground wires.

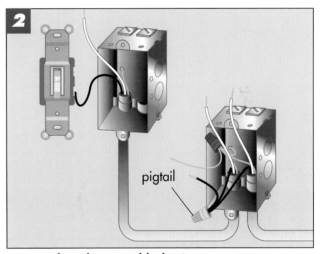

2. Attach and connect black wires.
Route power to the switch by tying the two black wires together with a pigtail at the receptacle box. Connect the black wire to the switch.

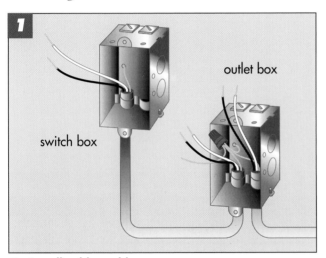

3. Continue wiring and split outlets.
Add black tape to both ends of the white wire that runs between the boxes to show that it's hot. Connect it to the switch and receptacle terminals. Connect the remaining black wire to the receptacle. Snap off the brass tab with needle-nose pliers to split the outlets. Leave the silver-colored metal tab in place.

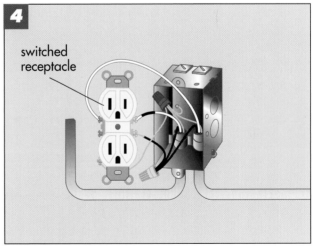

4. Complete the wiring.
Connect the white and ground wires to the receptacle, screw the receptacle and switch to their boxes, turn on the power, and test. In this example, the upper outlet will be live only when the switch is on. The lower one remains on at all times.

ADDING OUTDOOR RECEPTACLES

The easiest way to bring power to the outside of your house is to install a receptacle directly opposite an existing interior receptacle. If you need to place the outdoor receptacle elsewhere, see pages 32–35 for ideas on fishing the cable. Be sure that the interior receptacle box you choose has room for new wires. Check that you will not be overloading the circuit (see page 104). Codes usually require a GFCI receptacle with a weatherproof cover plate with a spring-loaded door.

YOU'LL NEED...

TIME: Barring unexpected obstacles, plan on 3 hours.
SKILLS: Basic electrical skills.
TOOLS: Drill with spade bit and perhaps a bit extension, screwdriver, lineman's pliers; a jigsaw, sabersaw, or keyhole saw. If you have a masonry exterior, a masonry bit, cold chisel, and hammer.

Drill at an angle to offset the boxes from each other.

1. Drill a hole to the outside.
Note: Be sure to shut off the power.
Remove the face plate and the interior outlet. To accurately locate your new receptacle, punch out a knockout hole in the back of the box, and drill a hole through the house to the outside. To make sure you have room for a box on each side (the wall may not be thick enough), drill off to the side.

2. Cut the exterior opening.
Find the hole on the outside of your house, and draw an outline of the new box (see page 26). Drill a hole at each corner of the box, and cut out with a jigsaw. If you have a masonry exterior, drill a series of closely spaced holes with a masonry bit. Knock out the hole with a cold chisel and hammer.

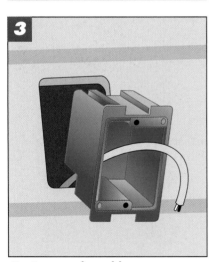

3. Connect the cable.
Cut a piece of cable long enough to allow you working room. Connect it to the interior box— you will need a helper to reach through the exterior hole and hold the locknut in position while you tighten the locknut. Connect cable to the exterior box, too.

GFCI receptacle

4. Make the electrical connections.
With the box pushed into place, strip the sheathing and the ends of the wires, and make connections on both ends of the cable (see pages 28–31). Be sure to connect to the "line" terminals on the GFCI receptacle and the load terminals on the existing interior receptacle.

weatherproof cover plate

foam gasket

5. Install the box and cover.
Attach the box firmly in place. With a masonry wall, insert screws into the back of the box and attach them to a framing member, or mortar the box in place. Fasten the GFCI receptacle to the box. Finally, attach the gasket and weatherproof cover plate.

INSTALLING OUTDOOR LIGHTING

*I*f you have eaves overhanging an exterior door, it makes sense to install a light there, where it will be better protected from weather than a wall-mounted unit would be. You're also likely to find it easy to run cable from an attic junction box to the eaves.

Consider installing a motion-detector floodlight. These are quite inexpensive, and if you wire it to be controlled with a regular wall switch, you can switch off the motion-sensing feature.

YOU'LL NEED...
TIME: With no unusual obstacles, plan on 4 hours.
SKILLS: Basic electrical skills, measuring and cutting eaves.
TOOLS: Screwdriver, lineman's pliers, drill, sabersaw or keyhole saw, fish tape.

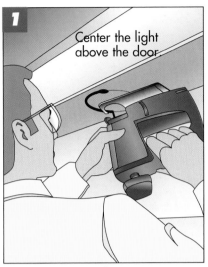

Center the light above the door.

1. Cut a hole in the eaves.
NOTE: *Shut off the power.* Draw an outline of the new box—a retrofit box with wings for attaching to the eaves will probably work best. Drill starter holes, and cut the hole with a sabersaw or a keyhole saw.

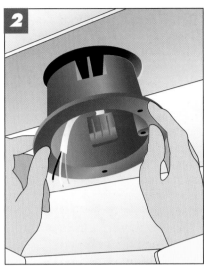

2. Run the cable, install the box.
Fish cable and make connections to an interior switch (see pages 36–38, 84). Connect the cable to the new box, and firmly attach the box to the eaves.

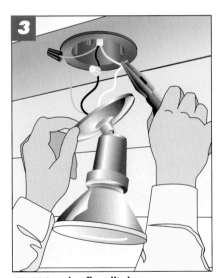

3. Wire the floodlight.
Connect the wires to the floodlight using wire connectors (see page 31), and screw the light firmly to the box. If your unit has a motion detector, wait until nighttime and adjust it so it turns on as people approach the door.

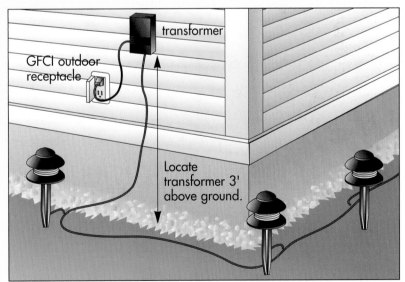

transformer

GFCI outdoor receptacle

Locate transformer 3' above ground.

INSTALL A LOW-VOLTAGE LIGHTING SYSTEM
For highlighting your landscaping, the easiest and least costly alternative is low-voltage lighting. Kits containing 10 or more lights, a transformer, and lots of wire are inexpensive and readily available. Installation is simple: Assemble the lights, and attach the cable. The lights usually can be poked into the ground, and you don't need to dig a trench for the wiring—just cover it with a bit of mulch. Fasten the transformer to a wall at least 3 feet above the ground, and plug it into an outdoor receptacle.

ADDING BATHROOM VENT FANS/LIGHTS

If your bathroom does not have a window that opens, most codes require that you have a vent fan to remove moisture and odor. Adding a fan can make your bathroom more pleasant, protect your walls from mildew and moisture damage, and can lower air-conditioning costs. You can wire a bathroom fan so that it operates by itself, but some codes require the fan to switch on with the light.

YOU'LL NEED...

TIME: About one day.
SKILLS: Basic electrical skills, carpentry skills.
TOOLS: Screwdriver, lineman's pliers, drill, sabersaw.

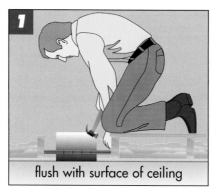

flush with surface of ceiling

1. Install the fan unit.
NOTE: *Shut off the power.* Cut a ceiling opening between joists. From the attic, nail or screw the unit's mounting brackets securely to the framing. Make sure the fan assembly is level and flush with the surface of the ceiling below before fastening.

MEASUREMENTS

WILL IT REALLY VENT?

Many bathroom fans do little more than make noise because they lack the power to draw moisture through the ductwork to the outside. The larger the bathroom and the longer the duct, the more powerful the fan needs to be. When you shop for a vent fan, know the size of the bathroom and how long the ducting will be. If the salesperson cannot help you choose the right-size fan, open a fan box and check the manufacturer's instructions.

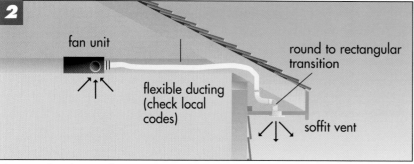

2. Run the ductwork.
In some climates, and if your attic has adequate cross-ventilation, you may be able to get by without venting to the outside—check local codes. Otherwise, run flexible ducting to a soffit or to a roof-mounted outlet. To increase the efficiency of your fan, run the ducts as straight as possible.

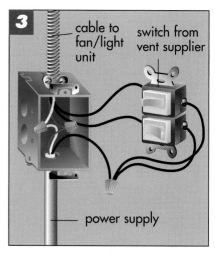

3. Wire the switches.
For a combination fan and light, fish two-wire cable to the switches, then run three wires from the switches to the unit. For a fan-only installation, run two-wire cable to the unit (for instructions on running wire in finished and unfinished spaces, see pages 32–38). If the fan has a heater, you'll probably need to run a 15- or 20-amp circuit (see pages 102–104 for information about planning and adding circuits).

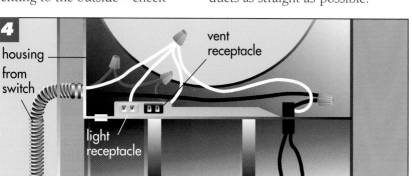

4. Wire the vent fan unit.
Inside the unit, connect the wires according to the manufacturer's directions. Typical connections are shown above. Install the working parts in the housing, and plug them into the appropriate receptacles. Turn on the power, and test the fan and light. Finally, fit the grille. Once a year, remove the grille and clean the fan blades and other parts inside the fan.

ADDING ATTIC FANS

On a hot summer day, the temperature in an attic can reach 150 degrees Fahrenheit or more. Turbine-type roof ventilators can help, but because they depend on wind to supplement the upward draft of hot air, you're out of luck on a still day when the heat buildup may be most intense.

A thermostat-controlled attic fan mounted in the roof or a gable-end wall automatically turns the fan on to vent overheated attics.

YOU'LL NEED...

TIME: A full day, with a helper.
SKILLS: Basic electrical and carpentry skills.
TOOLS: Ladder to get to the roof, roof jacks to provide a safe standing place if the roof is steep, drill, sabersaw or keyhole saw, utility knife, hammer, screwdriver, lineman's pliers.

Money $ Saver

COMBINE WHOLE-HOUSE FANS AND ATTIC FANS

Depending on your climate and use pattern, it may make economic sense to combine a thermostat-controlled fan with a whole-house fan. Here's why:
■ Even after sundown, super-heated air continues to put a heavy strain on your home's air-conditioning system. By improving attic ventilation, you can cut cooling costs by as much as 30 percent.
■ A whole-house fan will pull a strong, steady draft up through the house—and push air out of the attic—on those days when you choose not to use the air-conditioning. It is not, however, effective to use a whole-house fan while the air-conditioning is on.

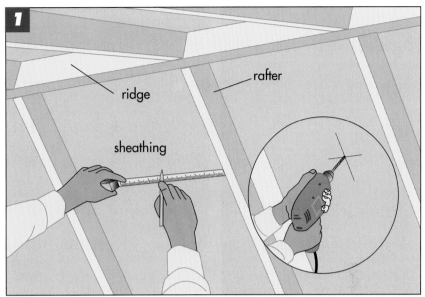

1. Drill a locating hole.
Position your fan as close to the ridge as you can so as little hot air as possible will build up in the attic area above the fan. Choose a slope of the roof that's not visible from the street. Go into the attic and pick a pair of rafters close to the attic's center. Measure to a point midway between them. Drill up through the roof at this point. Leave the drill bit in place or push a piece of wire up through the hole as a marker.

MEASUREMENTS

HOW BIG A FAN DO YOU NEED?

To determine how powerful a unit to buy, multiply the square footage of your attic by 0.7. Add 15 percent if your roofing is dark-colored—it will absorb more heat from sunlight than a lighter, more reflective roofing color. The resulting number tells you the cubic feet per minute (CFM) that your fan should pull.

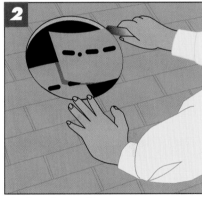

2. Cut the roofing.
Find the locating hole on the roof, and set the fan in place on top of it. The flashing should tuck neatly under shingles above the fan housing. To minimize the number of shingles you will have to trim, adjust the unit up or down slightly. Trace the outline of the unit on the roofing.

Use the template that comes with the fan to mark for a circular cut on the shingles. Cut the shingles with a utility knife.

For a gable-end installation, cut through the siding only—not the sheathing—with a circular saw. If the wall has a window or louvers, adapt the opening to fit the fan.

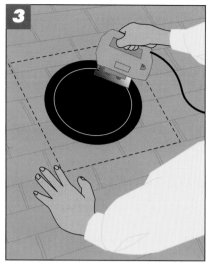

3. Cut the sheathing.

A second template will guide you in marking a smaller circle inside the cutaway shingles. Use a sabersaw or keyhole saw to cut through the roofing paper and sheathing. Remove any nails in the shingles that lie in the top two-thirds of the square you've drawn. Now you're ready to slip the unit in place.

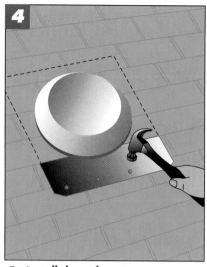

4. Install the exhaust vent.

Turn the fan over, and coat the underside of its flashing with roofing cement. Slide it under the shingles above and on either side; the flashing should overlap the shingles below the housing. Center the fan over the hole. Pry up shingles covering the flashing, and nail it in place. Drive the nails so they penetrate the sheathing, and coat them with roofing cement.

EXPERTS' INSIGHT

BUILDING A DEFENSE AGAINST HUMIDITY

If you live in an area known for high humidity, consider purchasing an attic fan that comes equipped with a humidistat in addition to a thermostat. A humidistat reads the humidity in the same way a thermostat reads the temperature, giving you another measurement for controlling the comfort level of your home.

On humid days an attic fan can make your home more comfortable by removing some of the moist air. Keeping attic moisture under control also helps keep your fiberglass insulation from compacting and losing its effectiveness.

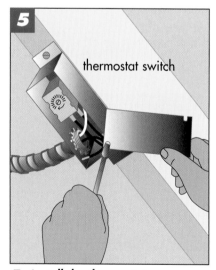

5. Install the thermostat.

Back in the attic, screw the thermostat switch to a stud or rafter above the fan and out of the airstream it will create. Remove the box cover plate.

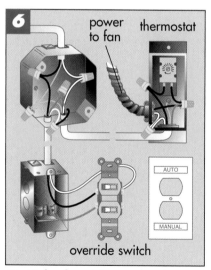

6. Make the wiring connections.

Run cable from a junction box to the thermostat. Install cable to an accessible switch that can be used to override the automatic control. Follow the fan manufacturer's instructions for wiring. If instructions weren't provided, make the connections as indicated above, using wire connectors.

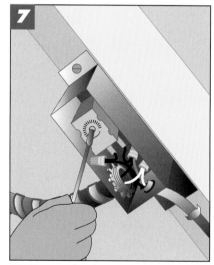

7. Test and adjust.

Turn on the power, and test your installation. An adjusting screw in the thermostat box lets you set the temperature that will activate the fan. The temperature setting will vary depending on your roof and the fan's capacity. Consult the manufacturer's instructions for the right temperature for your attic.

ADDING WHOLE-HOUSE FANS

Before you select a whole-house fan, plan the overall venting of your house. The fan should pull air through open windows and doors on the lower floors and out through vents in the attic, eaves, and gables. Without adequate openings below and above the fan, it will not be able to do its job. Leave at least 2 feet of clearance between the fan and any obstructions. If you stack your attic with boxes, the fan may not have room to breathe, which will make it noisy as well as inefficient. Installation is not as difficult as you may think: The fan sits on top of joists in the attic, so cutting and reframing aren't necessary.

YOU'LL NEED...

TIME: About a day, if fishing the cable is straightforward.
SKILLS: Basic electrical and carpentry skills.
TOOLS: Drill, sabersaw, screwdriver, lineman's pliers.

MEASUREMENTS

CHOOSING A FAN

■ Buy a fan that's rated to pull a minimum cubic feet per minute (CFM) equal to the square footage of your house multiplied by 3.

■ Do you really plan on venting the whole house? If you will open the windows of just a few rooms, use only their square footage to figure the needed CFM.

■ Often a hall is the best spot for a fan. Will it fit yours? Fans designed to vent houses larger than 1,800 square feet (5,400 CFM) generally have louver panels of 38 inches or more—too wide for some hallways.

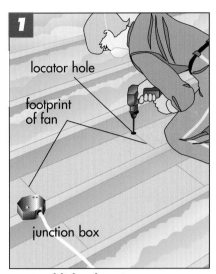

1. Establish a location.

Find a spot for the fan—the top-floor hallway ceiling is the usual place. Measure from a point common to the hall and the attic, choose a location for the fan, and clear away the insulation. Beside the joists, drill locator holes for cutting away the drywall or plaster. From below, cut a hole in the ceiling. Don't cut any joists.

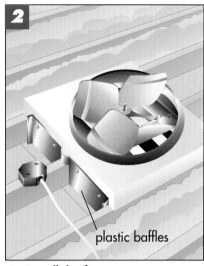

2. Install the fan.

Set the fan on top of the joists, directly above the ceiling hole. Secure it by driving screws into the joists. Fasten it down tight so it cannot vibrate. Install the plastic baffles provided with the fan. They seal the cavities between the joists.

3. Install the louver panel.

From below, tip the louver panel in place so it covers the entire hole. Attach it to the ceiling by driving screws up into the joists. The louver is lightly spring-loaded, so it stays shut when the fan is not in use but opens when the fan is switched on.

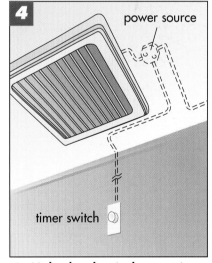

4. Make the electrical connections.

Run power up into a switch then to the fan (see pages 26, 35, and 84). Consider installing a timer switch so you can have the fan run during those times of the day when it is most needed.

INSTALLING DOORBELL INTERCOMS

With conventional intercom systems, you have to run bell wires from intercom to intercom. That can mean spending hours drilling holes and fishing wire or tolerating foot after foot of exposed wire running along the baseboards. Newer doorbell intercoms sidestep these problems by using a combination of existing bell wire and standard 120-volt power circuits to carry your two-way conversations.

For room-to-room communication, you can buy similar units that use only your electrical circuits and no bell wire. You simply mount the inexpensive units on a wall, plug them in, and start talking.

YOU'LL NEED...
TIME: Two hours to install a doorbell module and intercom.
SKILLS: Connecting wires.
TOOLS: Screwdriver, drill.

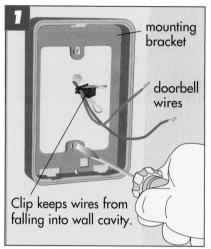

mounting bracket

doorbell wires

Clip keeps wires from falling into wall cavity.

1. Install mounting bracket.
NOTE: *Shut off the power.* Test that the power to the doorbell is shut off by pressing the button—the chime or bell shouldn't sound. Remove the doorbell button, and disconnect the wires from the terminals. Fasten the new doorbell mounting bracket to the wall with screws. Fasten the top screw first, check the unit for plumb, then insert the bottom screw.

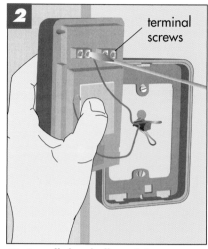

terminal screws

2. Install doorbell module.
Attach the bell wires to the terminal screws on the back of the doorbell module. Indoors, find your existing doorbell transformer (see page 63). Transfer the wires from its terminals to the new AC adapter that comes with the system. Plug the adapter into the nearest 120-volt receptacle. This links the doorbell module to the circuit that will carry the signal to the intercom monitor.

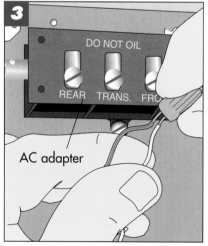

AC adapter

3. Disconnect the chime or bell.
Remove the doorbell or chime cover. Unscrew the terminal screws and remove the wires. Twist the bare ends of the wires together, and cover the splice with a small wire connector (see page 31). Replace the cover. The doorbell will no longer be used.

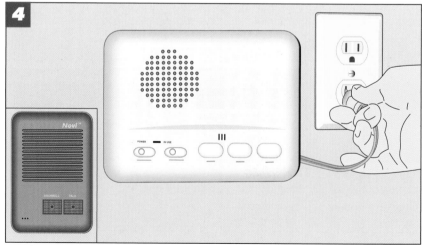

4. Plug in the intercom.
Choose a location for the intercom monitor, fasten it to the wall with the screws provided, hang the unit in place, and plug its cord into a 120-volt receptacle. Restore power to the circuit, and test the unit. Pressing the button on the outdoor unit produces a gong-like sound from the monitor. The signal is carried from the outdoor unit, along the bell wire, into the household circuit, to the intercom monitor, allowing you to talk with whoever is at the door.

INSTALLING VIDEO INTERCOM SYSTEMS

For a surprisingly small amount of work, you can install a video intercom that lets you see and hear the person at your door. For about the cost of a full-size television, this system provides a new level of convenience and security.

One of the simpler systems to install is wired by running a four-wire, 18-gauge cable from a camera outside to the monitor inside. The monitor plugs into a standard electrical receptacle. The toughest part of the job is pulling the four-wire cable from the front door to the monitor location.

YOU'LL NEED...

TIME: Several hours to install in most cases.
SKILLS: Connecting wires, running cable.
TOOLS: Screwdriver, drill, jigsaw, fish tape, wire stripper.

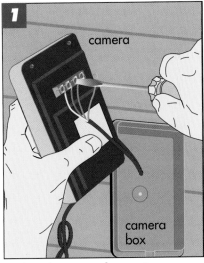

1. Attach camera box, wire camera.
Choose a location for the camera as close to eye level as possible. Cut an opening in the wall (see page 94) and run four-wire, 18-gauge cable from the box to the location of your monitor (see page 82). Attach the box to the wall; connect the wires to the terminals on the back of the camera.

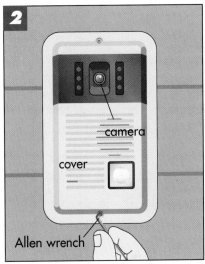

2. Install camera.
You may want to adjust the camera angle up or down if the unit cannot be placed at eye level. Place the camera unit in the camera box, install the front panel, and secure it with tamperproof screws. Tighten them with the Allen wrench that comes with the unit, and insert protective caps.

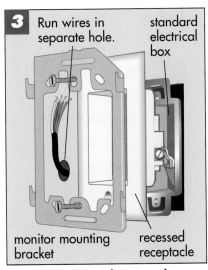

3. Wire a recessed receptacle.
A recessed receptacle (sometimes called a clock receptacle because it often is located behind electric wall clocks) allows you to install the monitor without having the electrical cord visible. Wire it as you would a standard receptacle (see page 58). Attach the mounting bracket for the monitor.

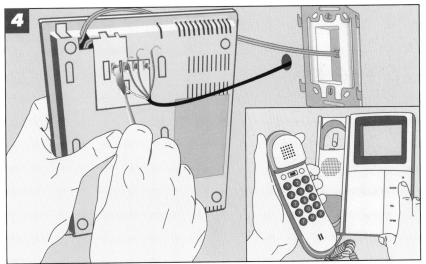

4. Wire the monitor.
Connect the four wires to the back of the monitor. Some units allow you to install electronic door openers. Plug the cord in. Push the monitor onto the bracket and pull downward to anchor it.

To operate the video intercom, the power switch must be on.

Adjust the volume and brightness controls. When a visitor presses the call button on the camera unit, you will hear a chime, and the visitor will appear on the monitor. Pick up the handset to speak. The visitor speaks through the microphone mounted on the camera unit.

PLANNING PATHS FOR NEW CIRCUITS

Electric cable often does not run in a straight line. Instead, it zigzags from one outlet to another in a circuit. Sharp turns and long trips do not bother electricity. You can snake cable up and down walls, along or across joists, and around obstructions without impeding the flow of electrons.

In this home, two general-purpose 120-volt circuits enter through the bottom plate of the stud wall and travel around perimeter walls to receptacle outlets. Two others go up into the ceiling for lighting and a 240-volt circuit follows along a floor joist to serve an electric stove receptacle.

Saving money by planning
Even though electricity isn't affected by bends and detours, cable is priced by the foot, and extra feet can add up fast—in extra labor as well as materials. So to be economical, keep your runs as short and direct as possible.

In new work, that's not too difficult. In this illustration of a well-planned new home, most of the cables travel directly to their destinations. The plan saved money by installing the dryer outlet near the service panel, minimizing the amount of heavier, more costly cable needed for its 240-volt circuit.

The plan also saved the electrician time, because there was no need for many bends in the conduit to carry the wire through exposed locations. For example, the cable for the 240-volt receptacle for the electric stove takes as direct a path as possible along the basement sill plate.

Drawing up your plan
In planning an electrical layout, especially if you'll be running more than one circuit, draw a floor plan of your home to scale, then mark the routes cable will travel. See page 12 for an example of circuits planned for one of the more complex areas of a home—the kitchen and family room.

To estimate how much cable you'll need, measure the distances involved, and add 10 percent for bends, unexpected detours, and waste. Be sure to add in another 6 to 8 inches to make connections each time cable enters or leaves a junction or outlet box.

Working in finished spaces
If you plan to fish through finished walls and ceilings, be prepared to use more cable than you would have to if the framing were exposed.

You'll also have some detective work ahead of you. Because cutting holes in walls and patching afterward takes so much time and effort, saving cable is a low priority when wiring in finished space. Search out the path that involves the least damage to your walls and the greatest ease in running the cable.

Your first task is to determine exactly what's in the space through which you want to run cable. If it's an exterior wall, for instance, there will probably be insulation, which makes fishing more difficult.

In addition, many older homes have fire blocking spanning the studs about halfway up the wall. If faced with these barriers, you will have to notch the wall surface at those points. See pages 26–27 and 32–35 for tips on running cable in finished spaces.

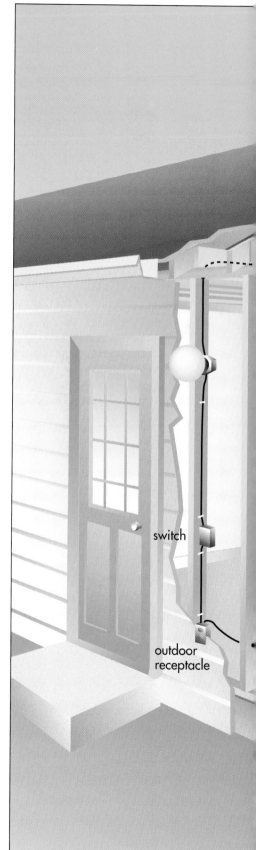

switch

outdoor receptacle

240-volt circuit
for electric stove

general-purpose
circuits

service
panel

junction
box

bottom
plate

branch
circuit

240-volt
circuit for
electric
dryer

PLANNING MAJOR CIRCUITS

Adding a new circuit to your home's service panel is an advanced project for which you may want to call in a professional —especially if your service panel is already crowded. Begin by seeing if you can add to an existing circuit. Failing that, make sure the service can be expanded. Look for an amperage rating on the main fuse, main circuit breaker, or disconnect switch. Older 60-amp service can't be easily upgraded; call in an electrician. Newer 100-amp service may have enough reserve to handle a new circuit or two, and 150- or 200-amp service usually has plenty of capacity.

YOU'LL NEED...

TIME: After running the cable to the service panel, 3 hours.
SKILLS: Understanding of electrical principles, general electrical skills.
TOOLS: Voltmeter, basic electrician's tools.

2. Estimate capacity needed.
If you can't add to an existing circuit, check the chart at right for the capacity your new circuit is likely to require. Rooms like living rooms and bedrooms that have about 10 light or receptacle outlets require only 15-amp capacity. Ideally you should have one general-purpose circuit for every 500 square feet of living space. Some local codes require that lighting and receptacles be on separate general-purpose circuits.

The kitchen is appliance-intensive and needs at least two 20-amp circuits. A bathroom gets by on one 15-amp circuit protected by a ground-fault circuit interrupter. Circuits for the garage, laundry room, and workshop need 15- to 20-amp capacity.

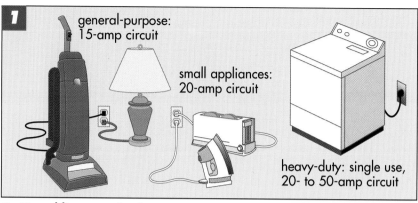

general-purpose: 15-amp circuit

small appliances: 20-amp circuit

heavy-duty: single use, 20- to 50-amp circuit

1. Try adding to a circuit.
Different circuits have different capacities. If your need for extra capacity is modest—a few extra receptacles for a bedroom, for example—see if you can add to a general-purpose or small appliance circuit. (Never add onto a heavy-duty, single-use circuit). Figure the total circuit load by totaling the demand of the appliances and fixtures (see page 12). Then check the chart at right to see if the demand is within safe capacity. The safe capacity of a circuit, as prescribed by the National Electric Code, is 20 percent less than maximum capacity.

CIRCUIT CAPACITY

Circuit rating	Maximum capacity	Safe capacity
15 amps	1,800 watts	1,440 watts
20 amps	2,400 watts	1,920 watts
25 amps	3,000 watts	2,400 watts
30 amps	3,600 watts	2,880 watts

CIRCUIT NEED SELECTOR

Location	Circuits
living and dining rooms, bedrooms, hallways, finished basements	A 15-amp general-purpose circuit for each 500 square feet. Separate circuits for lights and receptacles may be required by code. For a room air-conditioner, install a small appliance circuit.
kitchen	At least two 20-amp small-appliance circuits and a 15-amp lighting circuit. An electric range needs a 240-volt circuit. A microwave oven may need its own circuit.
bathroom	A 15-amp general-purpose circuit with GFCI protection.
garage	A 15- or 20-amp general-purpose circuit (depending on tools and machinery, if any), with GFCI protection.
laundry	A 20-amp small appliance circuit for the washer and a gas dryer. An electric dryer needs a 240-volt circuit.
workshop	A 20-amp GFCI circuit; for larger shops, run two 20-amp circuits or a separate circuit for lighting.
outdoors	One 20-amp GFCI circuit.

3. Check the total service capacity.

Now that you know what additional circuit capacity you'll need, can your service capacity handle it? If you add up the amperage ratings for all the circuit breakers or fuses, plus the circuits you want to add, you may discover that the total equals or even exceeds the amperage rating of your service panel. Does that mean you can't add new circuits?

Not likely. Few if any of the circuits ever work at full amperage capacity. And, some of your electrical fixtures and appliances never run at the same time—a furnace blower and an air-conditioner, for example. That's why codes allow you to de-rate your service capacity. De-rating is a standardized reduction used when computing service capacity. The chart shows a de-rating calculation for a 2,000-square-foot

3 — DE-RATING SERVICE CAPACITY

Formula		Compute	
Add		The first 10,000 watts at 100 percent	10,000 W
general-purpose circuits (square footage x 3 watts)	6,000 W	the remaining 13,500 watts at 40 percent	+ 5,400 W
small-appliance circuits (number x 1,500 watts)	7,500 W	De-rated total:	15,400 W
heavy-duty circuits (total of appliance name-plate ratings in watts)	10,000 W	**Divide**	
		The total de-rated wattage by voltage (240)	÷ 240 V
Total:	23,500 W	De-rated amperage	64.2 A

house with 100-amp service, five small-appliance circuits, and two heavy-duty circuits.

In assigning wattage values, don't count each general-purpose circuit. Instead, use 3 watts per square foot of house area. Small-appliance circuits rate at 1,500 watts each. Use the full wattage rating for heavy-duty circuits. If two items never run simultaneously, ignore the one that draws less. Rate only the first 10,000 watts of the total at full value, then calculate 40 percent of the remainder. Divide the total by 240 volts. The answer, 64.2 amps, shows that the system could accommodate more circuits.

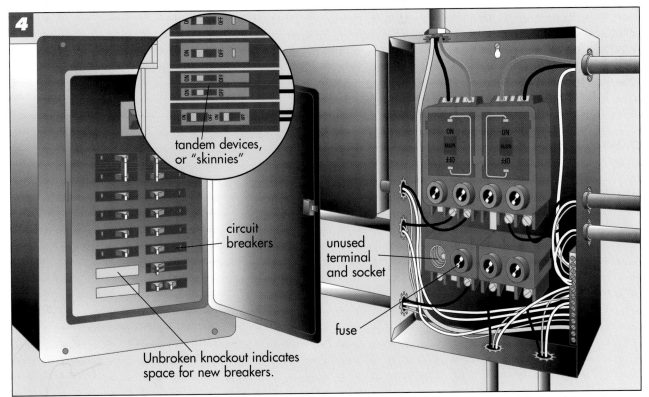

tandem devices, or "skinnies"

circuit breakers

unused terminal and socket

fuse

Unbroken knockout indicates space for new breakers.

4. Check for room in the box.

Once you've decided the type and capacity of your new circuit, see if you have room for it in your service panel. If your panel has circuit breakers, you might find a blank space or two. (Unbroken knockouts on the panel indicate space for a breaker underneath.) If not, you may be able to double up two circuits by replacing an existing breaker with a tandem device, also called a skinny. In a fuse box you might find an unused terminal and socket that could be used. More likely, you'll have to add a secondary fuse box called a subpanel (see page 107).

ADDING MAJOR CIRCUITS

1. To install new circuits, shut off power to the box.
Before working on the box itself, work backward from the new electrical installation. Mount boxes, connect them with cable, and run wiring back to the service panel (see pages 24–25, 32–45, and 84–93) in what the pros call a "home run." Next comes the serious business of adding and tying into a new circuit. First, look for your home's main disconnect switch. You may have a switch outside the house near the meter (as shown) or inside near the service panel. If you have such a remote disconnect, flip the switch or pull the fuse, open the service panel, and test it.

If your main disconnect is part of the service panel, seek advice from an electrician, an electrical inspector, or your utility company. To make sure there is no power coming into the service panel, you may have to ask the utility company to have the meter pulled and reconnected later.

EXPERTS' INSIGHT

Outdoor Shutoff Switches
■ If your indoor service panel is located more than 5 feet from the meter, an outdoor shutoff switch is required.
■ If you have an outdoor shutoff switch, it's a good idea to keep it secured with a padlock. Otherwise, anyone passing through your backyard can easily turn off the power to your entire house.

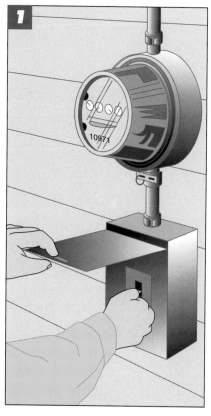

2. Test to make sure power is off.
Check that power is off, that main breakers are off, or the main fuses are removed. Stand on a board, rubber mat, or other insulator. Being careful not to touch electrical or plumbing fittings, remove the cover plate. Test the terminals of the main power lines with the probes of a voltmeter. If you've got a reading, there is power to that point.

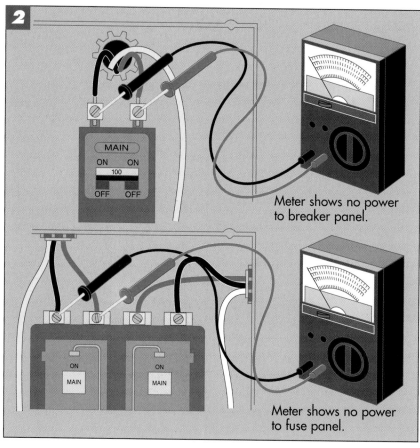

Meter shows no power to breaker panel.

Meter shows no power to fuse panel.

3. Hook up the new breakers.

Punch out the center from a convenient knockout on the circuit panel box. If needed, pry out one or more of the knockout's concentric rings to make a hole the size of the cable connector you'll be using.

Strip the cable sheathing, allowing for enough wire to reach the neutral bus bar as well as the blank space where you'll install the new breaker. Connect the cable to the box. Inside the service panel, run the white and ground wires to the neutral bus bar. (No ground wire is used if you are using conduit or BX.) For a 120-volt circuit, attach the black or red wire to the terminal of a single-pole breaker. To finish the job, simply clip the breaker onto one of the hot bus bars.

Some 240-volt appliances, such as water heaters, do not require a third neutral wire. For this type, connect two hot wires to a two-pole breaker (twice as wide as a single-pole breaker), and attach the ground wire to the neutral bar.

Most 240-volt circuits run a white, neutral wire and are sometimes called 120/240-volt circuits. Connect the two hot wires to the two-pole breaker and the white wire to the neutral bar. GFCI breakers install somewhat differently (see page 77).

4. Adding a subpanel

If you have a crowded fuse box or are adding several circuits far from the main service panel, connect them to a remote subpanel. Then make just one home run back to the main panel.

You will need a new panel with breakers or fuses, as well as three-wire cable with wire sized to handle the total amperage that the entire subpanel will draw. Connect the cable at the main service panel with terminal lugs.

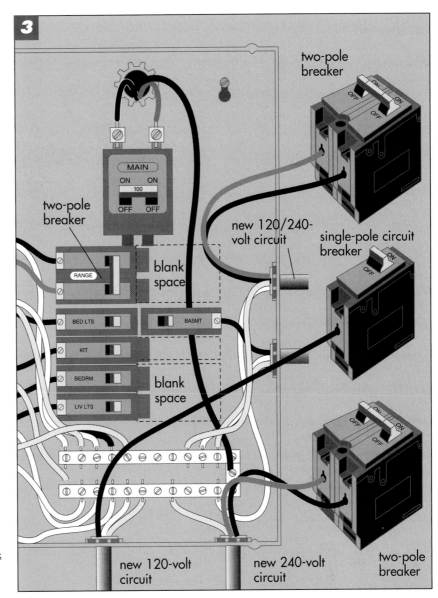

3

two-pole breaker

two-pole breaker

MAIN
ON   ON
100
OFF   OFF

RANGE

blank space

new 120/240-volt circuit

single-pole circuit breaker

BED LTS

BASMT

KIT

BEDRM

blank space

LIV LTS

new 120-volt circuit

new 240-volt circuit

two-pole breaker

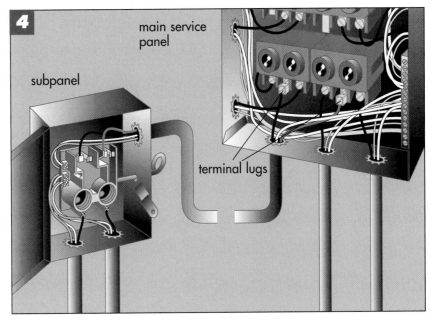

4

subpanel

main service panel

terminal lugs

GLOSSARY

For more information, refer to the index on page 110.

Amp (A). A measurement of the amount of electrical current in a circuit at any moment. See *Volt* and *Watt*.

Armored cable. Two or more insulated wires wrapped in a protective metal sheathing.

Ballast. Transformer that steps up the voltage in a fluorescent lamp.

Bell wire. A thin wire used for doorbells. Typically 18-gauge.

Bimetal. Two metals that heat and cool at different rates to open or close a circuit automatically. They are commonly used in circuit breakers and thermostats.

Box. A metal or plastic enclosure within which electrical connections are made.

Bus bar. A main power terminal to which circuits are attached in a fuse or breaker box. One bus bar serves the circuit's hot side, the other the neutral side.

BX. A trade name for flexible armored cable.

Cable. Two or more insulated conductors wrapped in metal or plastic sheathing.

Circuit. The path of electrical flow from a power source through an outlet and back to ground.

Circuit breaker. A switch that automatically interrupts electrical flow in a circuit in case of an overload or short.

Codes. Local laws governing safe wiring practices. See *National Electrical Code*.

Common. A terminal on a three-way switch, usually with a dark-colored screw and marked COM.

Conductor. A wire or anything else that carries electricity.

Conduit. Rigid or flexible tubing through which wires are run.

Contact. The point where two electrical conductors touch.

Continuity tester. A device that tells whether a circuit is capable of carrying electricity.

Delayed-start tube. A type of fluorescent tube that takes a few seconds to warm up.

De-rate. To lower total service capacity because not all the appliances and fixtures on a circuit are used at the same time.

Dimmer. A switch that lets you vary the intensity of a light.

Duplex receptacle. A device that includes two plug outlets. Most receptacles in homes are duplexes.

Electrical metallic tubing (EMT). Thin-walled, rigid conduit suitable for indoor use.

Electrons. Invisible particles of charged matter moving at the speed of light through an electrical circuit.

Fishing. Getting cables through finished walls and ceilings.

Fish tape. A long strip of spring steel used for fishing cables and for pulling wires through conduit.

Fixture. Any light or other electrical device permanently attached to a home's wiring.

Flexible metal conduit. Tubing that can be bent easily by hand. See *Greenfield*.

Fluorescent tube. A light source that uses an ionization process to produce ultraviolet radiation. This becomes visible light when it hits the coated inner surface of the tube.

Four-way switch. A type of switch used to control a light from three or more locations.

Fuse. A safety device designed to stop electrical flow if a circuit shorts or is overloaded. Like a circuit breaker, a fuse protects against fire from overheated wiring.

Ganging. Assembling two or more electrical components into a single unit. Boxes, switches, and receptacles often are ganged.

General-purpose circuit. Serves several light and/or receptacle outlets. See *Heavy-duty circuit* and *Small-appliance circuit*.

Greenfield. Flexible metal conduit through which wires are pulled.

Ground. Refers to the fact that electricity always seeks the shortest possible path to the earth. Neutral wires carry electricity to ground in all circuits. An additional grounding wire, or the sheathing of metal-clad cable or conduit, protects against shock from a malfunctioning device.

Ground-fault circuit interrupter (GFCI). A safety device that senses any shock hazard and shuts down a circuit or receptacle.

Heavy-duty circuit. Serves just one 120- to 240-volt appliance. See *General-purpose circuit* and *Small-appliance circuit*.

Hot wire. The conductor that carries current to a receptacle or other outlet. See *Ground* and *Neutral wire*.

Incandescent bulb. Light source with an electrically charged metal filament that burns at white heat.

Insulation. A nonconductive covering that protects wires and other electricity carriers.

Junction box. An enclosure used for splitting circuits into different branches. In a junction box, wires connect only to each other, never to a switch, receptacle, or fixture.

Kilowatt (kw). One thousand watts. A kilowatt hour is the standard measure of electrical consumption.

Knockouts. Tabs that can be removed to make openings in a box. The openings accommodate cable and conduit connectors.

LB connector or fitting. Elbow for conduit with access for pulling wires.

Leads. Short wires.

National Electrical Code (NEC). A set of rules governing safe wiring methods drafted by the National Fire Protection Association. Local codes sometimes differ from and take precedence over the NEC.

Neon tester. A device with two leads and a small bulb that determines whether a circuit is carrying current.

Neutral wire. A conductor that carries current from an outlet back to ground. It is clad in white insulation. See *Ground* and *Hot wire*.

Nonmetallic sheathed cable. Two or more insulated conductors clad in a plastic covering.

Outlet. Any potential point of use in a circuit, including receptacles, switches, and light fixtures.

Overload. When a circuit is carrying more amperage than it was designed to handle. Overloading causes wires to heat up, which in turn blows fuses or trips circuit breakers.

Polarized plugs. Plugs designed so the hot and neutral sides of a circuit can't be accidentally reversed. One prong of the plug is a different shape than the other.

Raceway wiring. Surface-mounted channels for extending circuits.

Rapid-start tubes. Fluorescent tubes that light up almost instantly.

Receptacle. An outlet that supplies power for lamps and other plug-in devices.

Rigid conduit. Wire-carrying metal tubing that can be bent only with a special tool.

Romex. A trade name for nonmetallic-sheathed cable.

Service entrance. The point where power enters a home.

Service panel. The main fuse or breaker box in a home.

Short circuit. A condition that occurs when hot and neutral wires contact each other. Fuses and breakers protect against fire, which can result from a short.

Small-appliance circuit. Usually has only two or three 20-amp receptacle outlets.

Solderless connectors. Screw-on or crimp-type devices to join two wires.

Stripping. Removing insulation from wire or sheathing from cable.

Stud. An electrical connector. (Also a term referring to a framing member.)

Subpanel. A smaller, subsidiary fuse or breaker box.

System ground. A wire connecting a service panel to the earth. It may be attached to a main water pipe or to a rod driven into the ground.

Three-way switch. Operates a light from two locations.

Time-delay fuse. A fuse that does not break the circuit during the momentary overload that can happen when an electric motor starts up. If the overload continues, this fuse blows, as does any other.

Transformer. A device that reduces or increases voltage. In home wiring, transformers step down current for use with low-voltage equipment such as thermostats and doorbell systems.

Travelers. Two of the three conductors that run between switches in a three-way installation.

Underwriters knot. A knot used to secure wires in a lamp socket.

Underwriters Laboratories (UL). Independent testing agency that examines electrical components for safety hazards.

Volt (V). A measure of electrical pressure. Volts × amps = watts.

Voltmeter. A device that measures voltage in a circuit and performs other tests.

Wall box. A rectangular enclosure for receptacles and switches. See *Junction box*.

Watt (W). A measure of the power an electrical device consumes. See *Amp*, *Kilowatt*, and *Volt*.

INDEX

G–I

Greenfield (flexible metal conduit), 19, 40, 41
Ground-fault circuit interrupters (GFCIs)
  breakers, 76, 77
  installing, 77
  purpose of, 10, 76
  receptacles, 10, 18, 76, 77, 94
Grounding
  methods, 10, 31
  purpose of, 6
  testing receptacles for, 59
Incandescent fixtures, 53
Insulation
  in incandescent fixtures, 53
  stripping, 28–29
Intercom systems, 100–101

J–L

Junction boxes
  for conduit, 42
  new installation, 22
  retrofitting, 22
    in unfinished space, 25
Knob-and-tube wiring, 11
Lampposts, 47
Lamps
  cord dimmers, 75
  rewiring, 52
  socket replacement, 51
LB fittings, 46
Light fixtures. *See also* Ceiling fixtures
  boxes, 22
  checking, 53
  fluorescent, 54–55
  incandescent, 53
  outdoor, 47, 95
  recessed, 70–71
  sconces, 72
  switch testing and replacement, 57
  track, 69
  under-cabinet, 73
  wiring, 84–90
Load sheets, 13
Low-voltage systems
  doorbells, 63
  outdoor, 95
  under-cabinet lighting, 73

M–O

Meter, electric, 6, 7
Motion-sensor (security) switches, 17, 74
Nail plates, 36
National Electrical Code, 4, 13
Neon testers, 14, 56
Offset connectors, 42
Offsets in conduit, 43
Outdoor electricity
  lighting installation, 95
  receptacles, 94
  running wires for, 46–47
  underground feed (UF) cable, 19, 46
Outlets. *See also* Receptacles; Switches
  testing, 13, 14
  types of, 6
  ungrounded and unpolarized, 11
Overloads, 8, 61, 62

P–R

Permits, 4
Pigtails, 31
Pilot-light switches, 17, 74
Plugs
  altering prongs on, 10
  replacing, 49, 50
  types of, 48
Polarization, 10, 59
Programmable switches, 17, 75
Programmable thermostat installation, 67
Pulling elbows, 42
Pullout blocks, 9
Raceway wiring, 78–79
Receptacles
  adding, 91–92, 94
  analyzers, 15, 59
  box placement, 24
  ground-fault circuit interrupters, 10, 18, 76, 77, 94
  grounding, 10, 31
  outdoor, 46, 94
  polarized, 10

  replacing, 18, 58
  splitting, 93
  surge-protecting, 60
  switch/receptacle, 17, 18, 21
  testing, 58–59
  240-volt, 18, 92
  types of, 18
Recessed ceiling lights, 70–71
Remote-controlled systems
  doorbell chimes, 65
  under-cabinet lighting, 73
Rocker switches, 16

S

Saddle clamps, 39
Sconces, wall, 72
Service heads, 6, 7
Service panels
  adding circuits to, 105, 106–107
  anatomy of, 8, 9
  outdoor shutoff switches, 106
  purpose of, 6
  safety considerations, 13, 106
  subpanels, 107
  surge arresters, 60
Shorts, 8, 11, 61, 62
"Skinnies," 105
Soldering, 15, 31
Surface-mounted wiring, 78–79
Surge protection, 60
Switches
  box placement, 24
  dimmer, 16, 74, 75, 88
  double, 16, 75
  fixture-mounted, 57
  four-way, 16, 90
  grounding, 31
  installing special, 74–75
  replacing, 57
  switch/receptacle, 17, 18, 21, 56
  testing, 56
  three-way, 16, 56, 87–89
  types of, 16, 17
  for under-cabinet lighting, 73
  wiring for ceiling fixtures, 84–90
Switch/receptacle boxes and switches, 17, 18, 21, 56

METRIC CONVERSIONS

U.S. UNITS TO METRIC EQUIVALENTS			METRIC UNITS TO U.S. EQUIVALENTS		
To Convert From	Multiply By	To Get	To Convert From	Multiply By	To Get
Inches	25.4	Millimetres	Millimetres	0.0394	Inches
Inches	2.54	Centimetres	Centimetres	0.3937	Inches
Feet	30.48	Centimetres	Centimetres	0.0328	Feet
Feet	0.3048	Metres	Metres	3.2808	Feet
Yards	0.9144	Metres	Metres	1.0936	Yards
Miles	1.6093	Kilometres	Kilometres	0.6214	Miles
Square inches	6.4516	Square centimetres	Square centimetres	0.1550	Square inches
Square feet	0.0929	Square metres	Square metres	10.764	Square feet
Square yards	0.8361	Square metres	Square metres	1.1960	Square yards
Acres	0.4047	Hectares	Hectares	2.4711	Acres
Square miles	2.5899	Square kilometres	Square kilometres	0.3861	Square miles
Cubic inches	16.387	Cubic centimetres	Cubic centimetres	0.0610	Cubic inches
Cubic feet	0.0283	Cubic metres	Cubic metres	35.315	Cubic feet
Cubic feet	28.316	Litres	Litres	0.0353	Cubic feet
Cubic yards	0.7646	Cubic metres	Cubic metres	1.308U	Cubic yards
Cubic yards	764.55	Litres	Litres	0.0013	Cubic yards

To convert from degrees Fahrenheit (F) to degrees Celsius (C), first subtract 32, then multiply by 5/9.

To convert from degrees Celsius to degrees Fahrenheit, multiply by 9/5, then add 32.